THE ITALIAN
MERCHANT
in the
MIDDLE AGES

By *Armando Sapori*

THE ITALIAN
MERCHANT
in the
MIDDLE AGES

Translated by Patricia Ann Kennen

W · W · NORTON  & COMPANY · INC ·
NEW YORK

FIRST EDITION

Translation Copyright © 1970 by W. W. Norton & Company, Inc. All
rights reserved. Originally published as *Le Marchand Italien au Moyen-
Âge* by École Pratique des Hautes Études, Sixth Section, Paris. Published
simultaneously in Canada by George J. McLeod Limited, Toronto.
Library of Congress Catalog Card No. 75-116126. Printed in the United
States of America.

sbn 393 05417 9 *cloth*
sbn 393 09956 3 *paper*

1 2 3 4 5 6 7 8 9 0

CONTENTS

THE ITALIAN
MERCHANT
in the
MIDDLE AGES

Chapter One

A PORTRAIT OF
THE MERCHANT

IN THIS PORTRAYAL OF THE MERCHANT, that great actor on
the economic scene of the Middle Ages, we shall first of
all consider his attitude towards his country and his religion,
and then we shall consider his level of culture.

1. The Patriotism of the Merchant

Two facts must be taken into consideration as the necessary background to this study. The Italy of the Middle
Ages had been broken up into a great number of city-
states, which were often no bigger than the town itself and
a small area of surrounding countryside. The inhabitants of
these city-states were engaged in constant warfare, in attempts to destroy one another.

The Guelph-Ghibelline division was the most important
one. In the beginning it opposed the states that supported
the Emperor and those which sided with the Pope. It soon

caused friction within the individual city-states, friction basically caused by the differing political aspirations of individuals or groups. In the end it had no real meaning at all and was little more than a name given to the varying factors fighting to gain control of public affairs. There were also other less important divisions, like that of the Black and White Guelphs in Tuscany, which developed afterwards. Each of these factions had the strongest personalities of the town as leaders—men who knew how to stir up the people and lead them into fratricidal wars. We see, therefore, that a spirit of faction was a dominant feature in the Middle Ages.

We must not forget, however, that fighting stimulates the mind and develops the mental faculties. It incites all the possibilities of the human nature into action, and, although in doing so it may cause many mistakes, it does pave the way for the progress of mankind. Now, since I propose to be quite severe in my judgment of the merchant, in order to reveal more clearly his positive qualities, I should like to make it clear that he was very quarrelsome by nature. When he quarreled he not only used strong language, but also revealed that he had a very hard heart and paid no heed to blood ties. His disputes were often instigated by the most trivial motives and then would drag on interminably, almost always passing from the stage of reasonable discussion to that of personal invective and sheer insult. A common insult was *ille diabolus,* and the "devil" in question would retort: *ille peior quam diabolus est, est homo pessimus, blasphemator Dei et omnium sanctorum.* In this way, a simple lawsuit for the nonpayment of a debt would almost inevitably develop with the passage of time into an indictment for immoral behavior or heresy. When the various members of a family quarreled, their troubles were not discreetly concealed within the home, but were exposed to the light of day, proclaimed in the market square, and reported in public documents. To give an example of this I have singled out at random a legal agreement signed by Ser Buon Ristoro di Guerniero and kept in the state archives at Siena. Nothing could be a better illustration of how anger could create such turmoil and trouble within a family. We do not know why the two young brothers, who were their father's business associates in a commercial house in Paris in 1261, should have quarreled so bitterly. Nevertheless, one of them promised his father that he would leave France, and the other that he would never show his brother the accounts of the business, and neither would he give him any of the money that would have been due to him in the normal course of events. The two brothers swore that they would pay a fine of a thousand marks if they broke their word. We do know, however, why Simone di Ranieri Peruzzi expressed such a profound hate in his will. In this document one can read the most terrible curse that a father ever put upon his son during the Middle Ages, or indeed in any age: "May my son be cursed for eternity by God and by me. So be it. And if he is still alive after my death, so that I cannot punish him as he deserves, may the justice of God punish him for his infamy and his treachery." The reason for this great rage was that the young man, who was in business with his father, had taken some money from the safe and, through this act of rebellion, had compromised the political position of his family, who then had to yield to the stronger faction in the town.

I have said everything to the detriment of the merchant, and now it is time to see the brighter side of things. Can we really blame the medieval merchant for not considering Italy with patriotic feeling? Our only task, surely, is to show that he loved his town, that is, the minute native land that was allowed by the times and the circumstances. Here, for example, are some facts about the merchants of Siena, which are to be found in a letter sent to France on the 15th of June 1260, shortly before the Battle of Montaperti: "Giacomo, you must know that at the moment we are weighed down with work and great expenses because of the war we are having with Florence. This will hit our pockets considerably, you know, but we will reduce Florence to such a position that we shall never regret all the trouble we have been put to. May God keep King Manfred from harm, and preserve his life. Amen." It can be said that these are merchants who see the financial side of warfare and regret the expense, even though they do not hide their hatred for the enemy. However, these merchants did not just complain, but often, spontaneously and generously, put their hands in their pockets, and went to the battlefield too. It was in the same period that Salimbene dei Salimbeni, the head of a large business house in the city, offered the town the enormous sum of 118,000 florins and said that he was ready to give the same amount again when there was need. And he, the business magnate, shut up his shops and hastened to the battlefield, just as the humbler merchants did. In the above-cited letter one reads on: "And you must know that because of the war, the army, and the cavalry, we have not been able to deal with our affairs. Mino Pieri is in the army at Montepulciano, and so is Orrando Bonsignore." Now, Orrando Bonsignore was the head of the Magna Tavola, about which Chiaudano has given us so much information. It is no exaggeration, therefore, to think that all the shops were emptied, both those of the great merchants and those of the minor ones, for one can believe the information supplied by this letter, which concluded:

"All of us will fight both the people and the knights. And we will bring disaster and calamity to the Florentines this very year, if it be God's will."

It should be remembered that there were war casualties in those days too, although not so many, of course, as today, and a great number of merchants died. I have spoken of Siena, and I should now like to pay homage to Florence, which I have chosen as my second homeland. Arnoldo Peruzzi, head of the famous business house, met his death fighting against Henry VII. The following entry in the account book of his business house is a witness to this fact: "A hundred gold florins he took with him when he left for the war at Incisa, when the Emperor arrived; fifty-three florins were given to the bearers who brought him back to Florence and the doctors who looked after him; eighty-six and a half gold florins were spent on the burial of the above-mentioned Arnoldo, who died on the 23rd of September 1312."

This same tradition was carried on a considerable time afterwards by Francesco Ferrucci, who improvised as a military commander and who was stabbed to death by a hired assassin.

In order to present a decisive testimony of the medieval merchant's love for his country, I have spoken first about his sense of military duty, which could carry him to the point of death. There is also another proof of this patriotism: the creation of works of art, which were designed to make his native city as beautiful as it was formidable. Let us look at some of the monuments of our Italy (I say "our" because Italy has the same heritage as France). How many of these buildings owe their existence to the merchants! Churches and public buildings were constructed to bear witness to their feelings of freedom and grandeur, and great town houses in which eminent ecclesiastical and lay personages, princes, and sovereigns were received. Even the kings of France and the emperors of Germany were given hospitality in these mansions at great expense, surrounded by princely luxury, in a style so distinguished that it won the respect and sometimes even overcame the insolence of those lords who in their countries were confiscating the fortunes of their hosts' fellow countrymen.

However, if we want to really penetrate into the soul of the merchant, we must follow him on his trips abroad. On the other side of the mountains and the sea this complex man revealed another face and another heart. If at home he was quarrelsome, suspicious, and cold even in his relations with his family, when he was away from Italy he forgot any political rancor and drew closer to his fellow citizens, inspired by a sense of solidarity, which was based on both practical and idealistic considerations.

On the practical side, this solidarity was shown by the associations formed among the various business houses. I have already spoken in several of my studies of the agreement between the Bardi and Peruzzi families, thanks to which the Florentines monopolized the underwriting of the English throne. I have spoken of the agreement between these two companies and the Acciaiuoli, which resulted in a monopoly on the sale of wheat in southern Italy. This association had a great influence as far as Rhodes, where the Grand Master of the Order of Jerusalem used a loan of several thousand florins to restore the castle of Villeneuve and build fortifications. At the same time the island was exploited commercially. Communal living quarters were built, as well as huge warehouses and depots for storing oil. Roses were cultivated for making perfume. The same kind of coordination took place in Siena. The Bonsignori worked continuously with the Salimbeni for foreign banking operations, and with the Tolomei in Italy. Another example of their solidarity is shown by their behavior when their debtors went bankrupt. The best-established business house in the city assumed the handling of the bankruptcy for all the other companies without charge, whether they had business ties with them or not. It managed the case in court, dealt with the trustees, signed the agreement, and then divided the expenses pro rata among the creditors, giving each the net sum obtained.

From an idealistic viewpoint, the merchant's solidarity abroad was not limited to his own city. It was then, when he was away from home, that a great and sacred name first appeared—Italy. It was then that this name imparted a spiritual content to a unity which could not exist in political reality, but which was the promise, many centuries before, of what would exist. The merchants seemed, more or less unconsciously, to pave the way for the Risorgimento, which was to follow centuries later. With this profound love of their native country, the merchants anticipated the poets, but in a more concrete way, which complemented the abstract beauty glorified in poetic form.

I have said "more or less unconsciously." I must add at once that external circumstances gave a new intensity to this feeling, together with the common language and nostalgia for the distant homeland, and helped to develop a sense of unity among the Italians abroad. Undoubtedly this sense of unity was intensified by the hostility of the ordinary people around them and the way in which the princes persecuted them and periodically attacked the solid front of the "Lombards," as they were called in France. It is irrelevant that this name was often spoken with certain overtones of scorn, for it was the name given to the principal commercial streets of the great European cities where the Lombards had made their business centers. Italians can have some pride in the fact that these names have withstood the passage of time. We are all familiar with Lombard Street in London and Rue des Lombards in Paris, which I, being a sentimental man, went to see as soon as I arrived in Paris. Although it is very small and has a rather bad reputation, it nevertheless made an impression on me, but not such a great one as did the ancient church of Saint Julian-le-Pauvre, where the Italian merchants of old used to pray to God for the well-being of their businesses and their native land.

There are innumerable references to the persecutions suffered by Italians on foreign soil. There are many slanderous statements in the chansons de geste and among the chroniclers who have transmitted to posterity their testimonials of Italian perfidy. They speak constantly of the falsity and bad faith of the Lombards: "They are tortuous and inconstant when they speak in one way and act in another. They are like eels and morays, the tighter you try to hold them, the quicker they slip away." Another point is their greed: "They devour and ravage the wealth and fortunes of the people," and "the Lombard monster not only devours man and beast, but field and forest, mill and castle too; it drinks up the swamps and dries up the rivers." They also wrote about the Lombards exploiting the poor: "They never carry any money with them, nothing but a piece of paper in one hand and a pen in the other, with which they fleece the townspeople and then lend them back their own money. . . ." "With what they get from their loans they wallow in luxury at the expense of the poor. They are wolves who eat people."

There were many references to their pride. A common saying was "He's so fat and haughty that he looks like a Lombard." They were seen as treacherous: "Look at the

Lombards, they are not loyal, but are treacherous and full of tricks." Another of their failings was cowardice. When, at the Battle of Courtrai, the Constable Raoul de Nesle advised the Count d'Artois to retreat, or at least to pretend to retreat, the Count insulted him by shouting: "Good Lord, that's the sort of thing a Lombard would say."

These observations, which I have selected from numerous examples, were made by people who did not realize that the Lombards were the pioneers of a true civilization in Europe. They could not see that the day would come in which all races would reap the grain that the Lombards had sown. I have had no hesitation in repeating their last accusation—that the Lombards were cowards. It can have no reference whatsoever to those fighters whose valor was proved on the battlefields, which were unfortunately Italian. Their courage was also shown in those countless battles against the Infidels, against the Arabs, and later on in the Crusades in Syria and Palestine. If anyone has been wrong about them, it was not the ingenuous chroniclers of those periods, but the historians who have repeated and spread these groundless accusations.

They were persecuted everywhere—in Spain, England, and France. In 1277 Philip the Bold (Philip III of France), who was suddenly seized by a false religious zeal following Pope Gregory IX's renewal of the interdiction on usury, threw into prison all the Italian merchants, who had to pay considerable ransoms to recover their businesses and their loans. "It was quite clear," says Villani, "that the King acted as he did out of sheer greed for money, and for nothing else, for he settled the whole question by demanding 60,000 Parisis * of 10 sous apiece for each gold florin." When the merchants had paid this they stayed in France

* A coin struck in Paris, heavier by one-fourth than those of Tours.

and continued in business as before.

In 1299 and 1308 the merchants were imprisoned again, this time by order of Philip the Fair (Philip IV). By frequent devaluation of the currency the kings managed at the same time to do great harm to those who were creditors in the kingdom, especially the Lombards. In 1315 Louis the Quarrelsome (Louis X) forced them to choose one of four cities as their residence and imposed heavy taxes on them. These measures were renewed by Philip the Tall (Philip V) and by Charles the IV in 1316, 1317, 1320, and 1324. In addition to this, the merchants were repeatedly forbidden to export goods.

They suffered a harder blow in the November of 1329, when Philip of Valois (Philip VI) not only renewed the violent measures of 1277, but made them harsher as well. While the Italians were in prison, he sent commissioners to each judicial district in order to hear complaints against the Lombards, who were forced to return any money earned through usury during the previous ten years. They also had to submit to corporal punishment and fines at the King's pleasure. Finally, in the four months dating from January 1330, all payments due to them were suspended, and all their credits were reduced to three quarters of their full value. A merchant from Pistoia wrote at that time: "We have no money at all, nor anyone to help us by paying our court costs. And I am sure that when we are set free we shall have to pay a pretty penny." There was nothing to hope for from the local justice. To take one's case into foreign courts was to confront many difficulties in procedure and to undertake enormous expenses without having the slightest assurance of a fair trial, since pressure would be exerted by the nobles and the people were against them.

In order to deal with all these troubles, the Lombards

created a "solid front, which was bourgeois, regional and
Italian." Ever since the first years of the fairs in Champagne, each town had arranged with the masters of the fairs
to send delegates who acted for all the merchants of that
city. A good example of this is Florence, which sent its
richest guild, the Calimala, to represent the whole city.
This shows that there was some kind of solidarity, and
there were other indications even then of a true Italian
unity.

In 1278, when discussions were being held with the
French sovereign about the eventual return to Nîmes of the
merchants who had been expelled from that city, a merchant from Piacenza introduced himself with the title of
Capitaneus mercatorum lumbardorum et tuscanorum. This
merchant had received full powers from the merchants in
Alba, Asti, Bologna, Florence, Genoa, Lucca, Milan, Piacenza, Pistoia, Siena and Venice. Ten years later in 1288,
the *Universitas mercatorum italicorum nunindas Campanie
in regno Francie frequentatium* appeared. This same *Universitas* in 1295 concluded a treaty for safe-conduct with the
Counts of Burgundy on behalf of the merchants of Como,
Genoa, Lucca, Milan, Orvieto, Parma, Piacenza, Pistoia,
Prato, Rome, Urbino, Venice, and for all the Italian merchants in general.

If one bears in mind all the political vicissitudes that
caused so many of these cities to be rivals and enemies, one
understands why we value this unity and this delegation of
responsibilities so much. The feeling for the unity of our
peninsula was first felt in two regions, Lombardy (north
Italy as far as Venice) and Tuscany (Emilia to Siena).
Then, later on, it spread to embrace the whole of the peninsula from the Alps to Orvieto and beyond.

The merchant loved his country as a mother, and the

mother, in turn, did not forget her children. It was she who aided them wherever they went. She was always there, ready to give them not only spiritual comfort but also practical help. One can safely say that wherever a single bale of Italian merchandise was to be found, there was also to be found the political or commercial representative of several Italian cities. He was there, ready to threaten reprisals for the injustices inflicted upon the Lombards. With inexhaustible energy, this representative organized the living quarters for the new arrivals and was always ready to act as peacemaker when quarrels arose among the Italians. The Italian merchants abroad were not only protected by these people, who had what might be called diplomatic privileges, but they had another source of strength too, which was a constant reminder of their birthplace and which inspired the respect and admiration of the foreigners who surrounded them. I mean their gold coins, which were symbols of grandeur and wisdom. They were symbols of grandeur because the Italian coinage was worth more than all the others. It was a symbol of wisdom because in Italy, earlier than anywhere else, the importance and necessity of monetary stability was understood. It was seen to have both moral and practical reasons. It added to the prestige of probity and helped the flow of commerce. Because it was held in great confidence and because it was incomparably beautiful, it could dominate all the markets of the world, so that princes often invited Italians to strike the coins of their countries too. The much-admired Italian money carried, as a supreme symbol of its sovereignty, the emblem of the town, in addition to a symbol of the Catholic faith. The Ambrosino of Milan had on its face the word *Mediolanum* inscribed vertically between the two patron saints of commerce, Saint Gervais and Saint Protais, and on the other side there was Saint Ambrose, whose name was identified with the Creed and who was the patron saint of Milan. The Florentine florin had the image of Saint John, the patron saint of the city, on both sides and also the lily which was on the flags at the battles of Montaperti and Campaldino, the same lily that was boldly and victoriously flaunted in the face of the ambitious Emperor Henry VII. The coins of the Venetian duchy bore the effigy of Saint Mark, who was both the protector of Venice and the symbol of all those struggles against adversaries and enemies of the faith.

2. *The Religion of the Merchant*

Together with his love of his country, a deep religious feeling was one of the nobler aspects of the character of the Italian merchant in the Middle Ages, and it was also an instrument of strength for him. If one wished to confine oneself to literary sources about this point, then the chronicle of Giovanni Villani would be enough. This is the open and true expression of the soul of the merchant who wrote it. His work was conceived with religious intentions, which had been developed through a constant practice of piety. In 1300 Villani took part in the pilgrimage to the Holy City of Rome to celebrate the jubilee called by Pope Boniface. From that moment he threw himself with great confidence into the arms of God, "in the hope of which," he wrote, "and thanks to whose grace, I accomplished this enterprise, and not by my own poor knowledge." A short time afterwards he returned to Florence and took up his pen, moved by the need to set down his feelings in writing. "And so that our work be more praiseworthy and better, I ask the help of our Lord Jesus Christ, in whose name every work has a good beginning, a good middle, and a good end." The entire work is penetrated by such a strong religious feeling that the author sees divine intervention not only in the general outline of great events, such as, for example, the loss of a war, but he finds it also in less important happenings, such as earthquakes and floods, fires and bankruptcies, all seen as means by which God punishes those who disobey His laws.

When we pass from Villani to the mass of his colleagues, whose lives were dedicated to business only, we see that they began their books and accounts in the same way as the Chronicle. This is true both of personal memoirs and account books: "In the name of Our Lord Jesus Christ and His Holy Mother, the Virgin Mary, and all the Holy Court of Paradise, through their grace and mercy may we be granted the blessings of health and wealth, on sea as on land, and may our wealth and our children be multiplied. Amen." This tradition lasted into the seventeenth and eighteenth centuries, even though it had become only the mechanical repetition of a formula which could no longer have the deep meaning it had in the Middle Ages.

Having considered the merchant as an individual, we will now examine the groups of merchants who formed the companies and guilds. The individual thought he would gain divine favor with his simple prayers full of naïve emotion. The companies, however, went further than this by invoking heavenly protection for their enterprises through the practice of charity. In this way they both obeyed the Church's maxim and inaugurated a program directed towards solving considerable social problems. The burden of this was divided, according to their different functions, between the state and the confraternities, or brotherhoods, which could be religious or lay.

The state, which was naturally preoccupied mainly with public order, usually restricted itself to providing food relief. During the frequent famines, it was very careful to provide the poor with their bare necessities, which generally took the form of bread. The congregations established funds either through bequests or donations from the living and with these supported almshouses and hospitals to help the poor and the sick. The merchants, the producers of wealth, assumed the daily care of the most unfortunate in several ways.

At the side of the large strongbox where the company funds were kept under the surveillance of the head cashier, there was a smaller petty cash box, which was under the control of the apprentices, who had the job of distributing the money to the beggars who came for alms. On feast days and holidays the companies filled each member's purse with a certain amount of silver which was to be given to the poor. The amount given and its destination was recorded in the books.

The next point I am going to make reveals very clearly the merchant's basic attitude. Each time they drew up or revised a budget, a fund for the poor was created with some of the capital of the company. These funds were entered in the books in the name of "our Good Lord God" as representing the poor, who, in this way, were made partners in the company. When the dividends were paid, a proportional part thus went to the poor. In the case of bankruptcy, the poor, who had until then been partners in the company, were transformed into creditors. The sums due to them after liquidation were paid to the archbishopric or to charitable associations, and when this happened, payment was made, not in money, but by allowing them to have preferential rights over the use of certain lands.

The statutes of all the craft guilds contained the obligation to fulfill their religious duties and help the poor. If we take as an example the Calimala Guild of Florence, we can see that the first article of their statutes stated that they had to be Catholics and had to help the State to eliminate any heretical deviations. The second article fixed a series of days on which the artisan could stop working, in order to practice his devotions. The fifth provided for the representation of the guild at the most solemn ceremonies, the representatives to be chosen from the most exemplary members by virtue either of their wealth or their conduct. The fourteenth ordered certain lamps to be kept lit in the Church of Saint John and the complete illumination of the church when solemn high masses were celebrated there. It also provided for special alms for the poor and for the distribution three times a week of a certain amount of good quality bread. Each guild was the patron of a church.

The religious feeling predominant in these guilds is attested also by the articles against perjury, which was thought not only to injure the good name of the guild, but also to wound God and make Him punish the whole city. Blasphemers and gamblers were also treated severely. They were threatened with expulsion and the loss of the right to exercise their trade, for blasphemy and gambling were thought to be execrable, and gambling was thought to reveal a desire for money exceeding the limits permitted by God.

My last observations on good works and religion, a topic which I do not pretend to have exhausted, will be about a widespread custom whose origin is unknown, but which was soon approved by law. An offering was made every time a contract of sale or purchase was drawn up. In France it was called *denier à Dieu*, in Germany *Gottes-pfennig*, In Italy *Denaro di Dio*. This money served as a deposit, but it was always destined for pious works, not for the seller. There are even statutes which affirm its legal position, establishing that once the money was handed over, the Good Lord was henceforth considered as a witness, and the contract could not be modified nor broken: *nec moveri nec infringi*. In Florence in 1311 the one thousand pounds coming from these deposits were destined for the construction of the church of Santa Reparata.

I must mention, finally, charitable bequests made in the merchants' wills and, in particular, the pious foundations and the custom the heirs had of giving away any money that the dead man had acquired by usury. It should not be thought, however, that only businessmen left donations in their wills: most people did it, since they were afraid of being damned eternally. Therefore we are unmoved when we read of these enormous sums and these long lists of beneficiaries, interrupted by the constantly recurring formulae of the notaries. It was, I repeat, the normal thing to do, and the amounts varied with the social class of the donor. Philip Augustus, for example, ordered 30,000 masses to be sung during the year following his death, and the noble Jean de Grailly, 50,000.

However, there are cases in which the merchant showed a sensitivity that befitted his complex personality as a man of business, accustomed to a life full of trials and grief. Scaglia Tifi, who died in Burgundy at the beginning of the fourteenth century, provided in his will for chapels to be built, several altars to be decorated, and various other pious works to be done. He also ordered the Master of the Hospital of Saint Étienne to buy a quantity of *sargia* (a sort of heavy serge) or other warm cloth at the beginning of each winter. This cloth was to be made into clothes for the poor. Faced with this generous thought that not only were clothes to be given to those who had none, but also that care was to be taken over the quality of these clothes, we feel inclined to forgive this worthy merchant for many things, like the careful order he gave for the exact date of his death to be registered in the books of all the monasteries, so that the monks could find no pretext for not celebrating its anniversary. We can pardon the parsimony, close to avarice, that he showed when, fixing the number of those who would sing masses for his soul and the amount to be paid them, he specified that if one of them fell ill or lost his voice, his stipend would go to the one who took his place. . . .

The custom of making the heirs give back the money gained through usury was peculiar to the merchant of the Middle Ages. It was only when they had done so that the heirs could enter into possession of the main part of the inheritance.* They had to find the victims of the usury and would go to the Town Council, which sent town criers declaiming the message through the town, then to commissions of monks who decided *quid intelligatur usura*, that is to say, which of the actions of the deceased had been really reprehensible. These efforts were rendered almost useless by the difficulty and the slowness of the means of informing the people and by the complaisance of the ecclesiastics, who would often decide in favor of the rich, if it was made worth their while.

Most often, the heirs solved the problem by doing nothing and leaving the disagreeable duty of the final settlement to their own descendants. Sometimes the merchant made his own provisions and left names and precise figures, as did

---

* However, the merchant himself was also inspired in his conduct by the common belief that one could efface a sin by post mortem expiation. Amanlieu VI d'Albrecht, for example, left one hundred pounds Morlas to provide marriage portions for poor young girls, "those that he had violated . . . if they could be found."

the Sienese merchant, Jacopo di Angelo.

On other occasions the bishop took an active part. He seized the dead man's account books and then decided, with a sort of interested liberality, how much had to be donated, over and above that which had been bequeathed to foundations, in an attempt to keep the soul of the deceased from being engulfed in the eternal pit of Hell. And when the booty seemed really exceptional, the "Inquisitors of heretical depravity" did not hesitate to bring a lawsuit to prove that the *de cujus* had given himself to diabolical experiments. Whether their information was true or false was a matter of no importance. This was the case with the above-mentioned Scaglia Tifi, who was undoubtedly a devout Christian. It is said that he had wanted to die like Saint Francis, on the bare pavement of a church. Someone presented the story that he had preached abominable ideas about the nonsanctity of marriage, the harmlessness of incest, and so on. . . . In brief, the goods of this "heretic" were confiscated by the Church. And this explains, if one may say so, the zeal of the Inquisitor, the monk Mino of San Quirico, who attacked Tifi from the Florentine monastery of Santa Croce.

In discussing the medieval merchant and his religious sentiments, I have not tried to uphold a particular line of thought but have tried to reconstruct reality. I have therefore tried to give a picture of all the aspects of his character, his enthusiasm, his devotion, and his sincere piety, and at the same time, to describe emotions which he could feel genuinely at times, but simulate just as easily. I have tried to set this in the framework of the period, when the Church encouraged alms-giving, which acted as a corrective measure in a society in which the economy tended to develop very rapidly. By soliciting charity on a large scale the Church managed to redistribute great fortunes, when, at the same time, the motives of the many churchgoers were not inspired by spiritual forces.

3. *The Culture of the Merchant*

The thesis of Werner Sombart on the level of culture of the Italian merchant of the Middle Ages is very well known. His points of view can be grouped under four headings.

First, Sombart tells us, the merchant did not like or have much talent for writing. Nor did he realize how necessary it was to keep accounts. In the fifteenth century Leone-Battista Alberti advised warehouse owners always to have ink-stained hands, which meant that even the director of a large commercial house was as clumsy as today's schoolboy, who gets his hands dirty because he does not know how to hold a pen properly. . . .

Second, when an exceptional merchant did keep business records, they were nothing but "untidy jottings," in which the entries played a role similar to, but not greater than, the knots the peasants put into their handkerchiefs when they went to market.

Third, these same books, when they existed, were *deliberately* kept in a very obscure manner so that in this labyrinth of scribbles no one could understand anything except the man who had made them. And, Sombart adds, the total absence of any records that would have permitted a description or an evaluation of the capital is an undeniable and significant fact.

Fourth, there were never any exact accounts in these books: the business man who wearied of keeping records also made mistakes in adding, like a child. He used Roman or Arabic numerals indiscriminately and counted on his fingers or his joints.

I shall proceed to refute these four points with the aid of unimpeachable documents. No aptitude for writing? But the Middle Ages was a period when the passion for memoirs was pushed to the point of exaggeration. Everyone who knew how to write kept a sort of notebook in which he set down his personal memoirs. I shall speak of them again since they have been a precious source of information for posterity. On the other hand, all those doing business with third parties resorted to notaries for any transaction whatsoever . . . from the purchase or sale of a building to the pawning of an old suit, from the taking on of an apprentice to the commissioning of an artist to decorate a room with frescoes or do an altar painting. We have found thousands of pages containing thousands of notarized contracts to confirm this statement, a statement borne out, moreover, by the authors of the books of rules in the period. Messer Pace da Certaldo, an anonymous Genoese writer, and still others specify the proper forms to follow in correct writing.

Second point: the absence of account books or the existence of simple notebooks of memoirs. I shall illustrate the character of the latter when I discuss bookkeeping.

Third point: the obscurity of the entries. We can prove the contrary. When there was a bankruptcy, the books were entrusted by the commune to a college of syndics, who did their job without retreating behind a barricade of insurmountable difficulties. On this subject, the procedure followed on the occasion of the famous failure of the Bardi and the Peruzzi in Florence is of decisive importance.

Fourth point: inaccurate calculation. When I was preparing my edition of the account books of the Peruzzi, I checked all the operations done on hundreds of pages and took note of the errors. There were almost none in the totals or in the calculation of interests. Those errors that do appear cannot be attributed to an insufficient willingness to be exact, but simply to an occasional reversal of the figures, as happens today, or sometimes, very rarely, to the mistaking of a ten in Roman numerals for a five. Moreover, in operations that reached up to a million pounds, these errors were in the columns of sous and the deniers.

And finally, it must be remembered that it was in these books that the accounts of the entire world were kept, that here all the weights and measures were equalized, since each region, not to mention each city, had its own different system; and that in these books the enormous sums lent to the sovereigns were calculated.

I cannot deny that as regards education, the situation in Germany was as described by Sombart. In Italy, however, it was exactly the opposite, notably as concerns arithmetic. We find, for example, in Pegolotti's treatise, that the hyperper, a Byzantine coin of 41½ carats, corresponds to 30 shillings and $7\frac{2}{83}$ deniers for each florin. As this single example shows, if they carried their calculations out to such a fine point, it was not from a desire for simple approximations, but for exactness pushed to extremes. Nor is this all: as early as the thirteenth century they were calculating compound interest, which was known as *fare capo d'anno*. From year to year, the interest was added to the principal and yielded interest too. As early as the thirteenth century they calculated the expected total at maturity, which was called then *ragguaglio in un dì*, that is, the average maturity of the sum of several loans falling due at different dates. And already in that same century they were calculating discounts, not by the system we call practical or commercial, but by the system we call rational, which we have abandoned because it is much more difficult, although better suited to the nature of discounting and to commercial equity.

Sombart states that the system of double entry bookkeeping had the same importance in economic and commercial development as the Copernican system in astronomy. But if this lyrical affirmation is to be believed, one should conclude that in the Middle Ages the movement of capital or the course of business undertakings could not be followed. In fact, in the thirteenth and fourteenth centuries, the great banking and mercantile companies continued to make their bookkeeping entries by superposition rather than by juxtaposition. And it was only later that Luca Paciolo first presented in an organized text the elements of this new form of commercial notation. He did not invent this system; it had been outlined in preceding years. The truth is that bookkeepers in the Middle Ages had attained the same results, using methods that were effective but much more complicated that double entry gives with a simplicity of form permitting automatic verification.

It is when we make the distinction between the formal and the substantial character of the two systems that this emerges most clearly. When I consulted the books of the Calimala Company, I copied down each entry in our modern system of bookkeeping. At the end of this financial exercise, having figured the extent of profits and losses and having assigned both the one and the other to each partner, I arrived at the same conclusions as the old medieval accountants.

Alberto Tofani, a specialist in these matters, contends that the accounts of the medieval merchant-banker were kept by outsiders who did not belong to the business houses and that accountants constituted a separate guild. What I have just been saying would in that case have very little value in assessing the technical knowledge of the merchant-banker. It has been shown, however, that this guild of specialized accountants never existed. In the Middle Ages the accountant was sometimes a professional, but much more often it was the merchant himself who kept his own books. The companies of the Bardi and the Peruzzi did use accounting secretaries (we would say today "head accountants"), but at the same time many of the partners, from the directors on down, personally kept either the primary or the secondary books.

The town's school was the starting point for the merchant in acquiring the skills we have just been discussing, and it was he who founded these schools for this purpose. If we look back to the earliest reestablishment of settled society after the barbarian invasions, we see that the merchant was the first to feel a need for elementary learning, which could only be satisfied by the clergy, since all that had survived of the ancient world was the exclusive patrimony of the Church. The men of the Church interested themselves in commerce too, either directly or by writing letters for the professional merchants, for pay or for a share of the profits. In that way the word "clerk" came to have its present meaning in all the Romance languages, while the word "diacre" or "deacon" had the same evolution among the Slavic languages. However, the monastic schools presented inconveniences and dangers. A young man might decide, for example, to remain forever in the peace of the cloisters, without considering the disappointment he was causing his father. Sometimes his vocation was spontaneous, but often the maxim of the Church: *Homo mercator vic aut nunquam potest Deo placere* ("the merchant is a man who can hardly ever please God") awoke a doubt in the mind of the young man and made him decide to stay in the monastery. Many cases of this are attested in documents. The merchant, who was always solicitous of saving time, naturally considered those hours spent in the monasteries on religious teaching or choral chant as lost. He thought it more useful for the apprentice to learn how to keep books and to write a good business letter. And that is why the rich merchants, called *maiores*, *divites*, or *otiosi* in the documents, resorted to education at home, always with the aid of churchmen. In taking the ecclesiastics out of the monastery and giving them a personal remuneration, the merchant prevented them from being the arbiters of the program of study. Later, laymen who had been educated in the church schools took over this job. They promised to teach their pupils (and this we know from notarized documents) how to interpret a contract or notarized document (*ut sciat leger instrumenta*), how to write a letter in the *volgare* ("vernacular") (*scripturas facere breves*), and how to keep accounts (*quod sit sufficiens pro scribendo in quadam apotheca pro scriba*).

At the same time, the communes were starting to take form, with the merchants in the positions of leadership. The problem of education became even more vital and gave rise to a conflict with the ecclesiastical authorities. The commune insisted on a lay school (or a state school as we would say today), while the Church did not want to relinquish its most potent instrument for shaping young minds. The political authority gained the victory and was itself confronted with the problem of professional education. We need only cast an eye over some of the thirteenth and fourteenth century documents to see the different styles of handwriting then in use. There were three of them and each one reflects a certain method of teaching and a certain mentality. The elegant chancellery style was perfectly suited to the solemnity and the finesse with which high officials treated questions of public interest. The notarial style, contorted, full of abbreviations and contractions, reflected the image of judicial chicanery. The commercial style, which was not without flourishes although lacking in superfluous elements, was strong in its strokes and clear in the composition of the page. This writing also reveals the character of the penman, that is to say: strong, reliable, and with excellent taste.

In 1338 Giovanni Villani wrote about Florence: "There are about 8 to 10,000 boys and girls who are learning to read; about 1000 to 1200 children in six schools are learning their ABCs and mathematics; about 550 to 600 are studying grammar and logic in four schools." After school there was university for the wealthiest, among whom there were certain merchants.

The schoolboys were lively, ready to argue and fight with stones, copying their fathers, who fought bloodier battles. But they also knew how to be good and generous. The teachers, whose names were preceded by the word *Ser* (an honorary title indicating respect for the "man of culture"), possessed all the characteristic traits of intellectuals, a ready wit and a critical mind, which was applied to the social, political, and religious problems of their times. We have an example of this which, although not frequent, was not unique. A certain Florentine, Gaspare de Ricco, who was a teacher in the school on the Street of the Ghibellines, was condemned to wear the yellow cross of the heretic; he had taken an active part in the revolt of the Ciompi,* was named

---

* In 1378 workers unaffiliated with the guilds took over the city, which they ruled for four years.

assistant to the people's notary, and later exiled.

As we have seen, the future merchant learned the basic elements of his technical training in classes provided by the commune. But the theory had to be supplemented by the practical training. That is why another type of training was organized, which I shall call "the workshop."

It was in the workshop that the education of those who wanted to specialize in industry and banking was completed. It was there that the apprentice learned the secrets of the trade and sometimes achieved not only the corporative grade of master but also the renown that comes to a great craftsman. It was there that he perfected his learning by making it practical. Gradually a great feeling for business was born in him. To appreciate the benefits that he could draw from this type of schooling, we must realize that the workshop fundamentally constituted a great center of life in the Middle Ages. The postal service which the mercantile companies provided for jointly, each one taking its turn, is an example of this. When a messenger was leaving for foreign parts, the merchants gathered together to give him their letters; when the courier returned, they arrived in crowds to get their replies. Obviously these letters were not read in public; one does not give away business secrets. But some of them contained news of politics. Information was exchanged; very often discussions took place; events were commented on; and the game of forecasting sharpened young minds. These periodic get-togethers gave the merchant the opportunity to extend his knowledge of foreign events—a knowledge that greatly influenced the growth of the economy.

Discussions and conferences took place in a certain part of the workshop, away from the curiosity of the customers. At the very back of the shop there was a corner reserved for the management, very carefully guarded from the interested glances of rivals and outsiders. There the clerk or clerks worked at entering the accounts in a number of ledgers that they pulled out from a large cupboard. Around them, boys were concentrating on learning the skills of accounting and calculating. What a marvel it would be to us today, accustomed as we are to the clacking of typewriters in modern offices, to follow the work of the medieval clerks and apprentices! The mathematical operations were performed on a checkered table (*scacchiere*) and on tablets that were ruled off into squares, on to which quick hands were continually placing counters. These movements corresponded in a way to those that our modern computers make mechanically.

The results were read out to the clerks, who wrote them down temporarily in Arabic numerals on slips of paper. They were then checked over carefully and finally entered in the account books, according to the rules, in Roman numerals. Handbooks of mathematical tables, called *manuali di mercatura*, made calculating easier.

It must be added that the Italian merchant of the Middle Ages not only knew a lot about his own profession, but was sometimes endowed with a literary taste and a real aptitude for belles-lettres. I shall limit my documentation to the city of Florence, although it might be more widely extended; but it will not be any the less conclusive for that, since there are a wealth of references for this modest-sized city. The Florentine chroniclers, Compagni and Villani, were merchants. Dino Compagni, a good-hearted and gentle man, was inscribed on the rolls of the guild of *Por Santa Maria*; at his death he left, in addition to a well-managed business, that precious manuscript that has been so useful in understanding Dante's poem. Giovanni Villani at the age of twenty-five was associated with the Peruzzi. After that, from 1324 on, he was associated with the Bonaccorsi company. His brother Matteo also belonged to the Bonaccorsi company, where he followed in the footsteps of his older brother until 1363. A little later he seems to have lived in Naples, where he continued to work for the same company, and for ten years in Avignon. The third brother, Filippo, took Giovanni's place in the Peruzzi company and directed their branch in Avignon. So they were merchants, all three, and descended from a family of merchants. Their father, old Stoldo, had belonged to the company of the Cherchi-Neri in the woolen guild. The practice of commerce was transmitted from father to son, in Florence and elsewhere, and it constituted a nobility as high as that with a blazon. In Siena in 1268 the Guidi company were bankers to the commune of Fermo. At its head was Francesco, son of a certain Guidalotto whose name appears on a great number of contracts made toward the middle of the century in Marseilles, at the fairs of Champagne, and in England. Another Florentine chronicler, Marchionne di Coppo Stefani, was the son of a merchant associated with the Acciaiuoli. Other less important figures, Simone della Tosa, Guido Monaldi, and Luca da Panzano, also lived in the fourteenth century; their journals and fragments of chronicles had the honor of being printed. Among the writers of journals also published in the fifteenth century, we can mention the apothecary Luca Landucci, the wine merchant Bartolomeo di Michele del Corazza, the coppersmith Bartolomeo Masi, and spanning the fourteenth and fifteenth centuries, the silk merchant Goro Dati. Finally there was Bonaccorsi Pitti, who, as he himself recounted, had spent his youth *trafficando e giocando*, and without a doubt playing more than trading, so that he became the prototype of the modern gambler.

In summing up, we can safely say that through their works the Italian merchants created the "historical archives of their cities." They were very well-known personalities. One can have even less doubt when I add the name of Giovanni Boccaccio, who handled some business affairs in Naples for the Bardi family, although it must be said that he was less successful as a businessman than as a writer. And then the name of Franco Sacchetti, who in his *Sermoni* has left us much useful and valuable information, the fruit of his great experience. These men were men of the first order, but still not exceptional. If, for example, the authors of the letters from Siena in the thirteenth century had had the same width of vision as a Compagni or a Villani, they would have left us texts as important as those of the Florentine chroniclers.

The Italian merchants brought civilization everywhere and opened the way to future progress without resorting to the use of violence and warfare. They prevailed through their audacity, sustained by a subtle intuition and by high moral values: love of their country, religious faith, and culture. There is nothing, I believe, more appropriate for establishing through the centuries their immortal spirit than these lines which are to be found at the head of a *Breve dell'arte dei Pittori* ("Breviary of the painters' guild of Siena"): "No enterprise, however small, can have a beginning or an end without these three characteristics: power, knowledge, and with love, will."

Thanks to this teaching, the Italian merchant of the Middle Ages traced for individuals and peoples of all times to come the only way that leads to a full realization of humanity.

Chapter Two

THE MERCHANT
AT WORK

IN THE FIRST CHAPTER I gave a general portrait of the merchant and showed how he stood at the center of international trade in the Middle Ages. I shall now discuss international trade in the Middle Ages, referring to the most essential features, the amassing of capital for the long-distance operations, the routes and means of communication, and finally the goods most commonly traded.

Before starting I should like to make some comments about the observations of Werner Sombart in order to refute any misconceptions that may have been created. Werner Sombart has simplified the economy of the whole of Europe and reduced it to make it conform to the limited economic development of central Europe. In addition to this he has, in my opinion, a basic error in his way of treating historical facts. He uses the present as a comparative measure for evaluating the past, especially when it is a question of figures. In this way the economic activity of medieval Europe is considerably reduced for those who compare the powerful liner to the heavy and relatively small medieval galley which was rowed across stormy seas, or the long goods trains to the carts pulled along by oxen, asses, or, when there were any, horses. In this kind of comparison not only does the volume of traffic seem ridiculous, but also the speed, if we compare the modern airplane flying through the clouds to the medieval traveler toiling over hills, through winding mountain passes and forests, with the danger of attack by ferocious wild animals, particularly wolves. He also had to face attacks from bandits, who infested the roads as pirates did the seas. An added danger was the intervention of the upper-class bandits, the princes and lords, who would attack both caravans and boats with an impunity denied to their equally dishonest, but generally more daring, rivals.

My own conception of the way to interpret historical facts is quite different. I agree that a scholar must not divorce the past from the present but I am just as sure, however, that he must try to understand completely the period he is studying in order to obtain a complete vision of the man of that era. In other words he must view things not only with his own vision as a modern man, but also see things through the eyes of the man of the period in question. In this way the historian feels not only with his own emotions but also with other people's and so can reconstruct with facts a living reality which still has a life force after the passage of centuries and which is not merely a mirror of death. The great master, Henri Pirenne, said that the historian "doit donner le sens de la vie." If he does not do this, he is only a skilled technician dissecting a corpse, or an antiquary collecting and dusting curiosities and arranging them far away from human contact, depriving them of life. If one accepts this, one is not surprised by Sombart. Sombart attempts to generalize the situation of central Europe and estimates the development of a medieval city using as an example a German city where, even in the middle of the fifteenth century, there were cultivated fields within the city walls. His picture of a medieval city is of a place where the noise of a flail used to thresh the wheat would disturb the artisans, where cows ambled up and down the streets, and pigs rooted out their filthy fodder there. But, in the same period, Siena, my native city, and Florence, my adopted one, had well set out, closely packed streets and could already boast of those monuments which are our pride and joy. Sombart took as his measure of medieval economic activity the movement of 293,760 marks in Lubeck in 1384. Much earlier—in 1318 in fact—the volume of business for the Bardi company alone had risen to 1,266,775 lira for that one year. In Venice in 1423 the volume of business was close to 10,000,000. One is not surprised, therefore, when Sombart speaks of numerous purchasers running after a single merchant who got into debt over two bales of merchandise, or of the total amount of goods crossing the Alps in one year as being no more than the freight one goods train could carry in one trip in 1922.

1. Capital and International Commerce

I shall now return to my original points for discussion and shall start with how the merchants got the capital to finance their trading operations. Usually they did not act singly, but in liaison with groups organized into juridico-economic associations. Naturally there were exceptions. Large amounts of capital could be managed by a single individual; we need only recall Floro of Salerno, who in the year 871 had such close business connections with the Moslem merchants of Media that he knew the plan of a Saracen expedition against the city. At the start of the Norman conquest Pantaleo of Amalfi made a donation to the archiepiscopal palace of his small, but already flourishing, commune of two carved bronze doors which had been cast in Constantinople. The Genoese, Benedette Zaccaria, having obtained toward the end of the thirteenth century the extraction rights to the alum mines of Phocea in Asia Minor, negotiated a monopoly, *in partibus infidelium*, and arrived at what economists today would call a vertical trust. He made arrangements to transport this precious raw material aboard his own galleys and established a dye works to exploit it at once. But these powerful individuals were the exceptions—partnerships were the general rule. There were two clearly distinguishable types of associations, which can be considered the first step towards modern companies. In coastal cities, where there was very little "hinterland" and the commercial activity was directed towards the sea, there flourished those associations known as *collegantia* at Venice and *commenda* at Genoa. When a boat was due to set sail, the captain or a third party was entrusted with a sum of money or some goods and was encharged with either buying specified goods or what was most suitable at the ship's destination, or to sell the entrusted goods and reinvest the money if he saw fit. The *socius stans* who remained on dry land only invested a limited capital in the transaction and took an agreed percentage of the profit from the *socius tractans* which could be lost.

In the inland cities, where industry and banking were prevalent, the type of association known as *compagnia* was most common. In these companies the members' personal fortunes were also at stake since they were held responsible for all and jointly with their fellow members in case of bankruptcy.

The first type of association, called *commenda* or *collegantia*, lasted for one trip only. The association was dissolved when the boat reached its home port again and the accounts had been rendered. Then a new association would be formed, sometimes with the same members, but usually with different ones. The late André E. Sayous was the great historian on this type of association. I should like to make one point clear, that the coastal association was not the only type, and that the inland association, the *compagnia*, or company, shows a continuity of purpose that merits notice. Obviously in different circumstances different kinds of associations were needed. With sea trade the principle of limited liability was recognized, after due consideration of the greater risk. (Boats could be lost through storms, fire, or piracy.) There was no solidarity among the members simply because they were members only for a limited length of time and were often strangers. Banking and industry, however, required a solid organization and imposed plans and commitments of longer duration, plans and commitments that could not be conceived, negotiated, or executed except by men whose contact with one another was more than occasional.

The mutual trust and long-calculated efforts which could reduce risks to a minimum and lead to happy results favored unlimited liability. In addition, a prolonged activity in common directed toward the same ends demanded of the members a reciprocal confidence and esteem and frequent consultation. It implied the other basic principle of the company; that of shared responsibility. This total solidarity in bearing responsibility conferred on the administration a particular prestige in its dealings with outsiders.

These types of associations had different legal bases, but their effect on the urban economy was similar. Werner Sombart is right to consider as absurd and ridiculous the pretension of calling any individual "a great merchant" who, in twenty or thirty years, executed a hundred or so contracts, each one involving on the average a hundred lira in farthings (*piccoli*). However, the diffusion of those contracts in many social milieux performed the same function in the economy of the great maritime cities as does the participation of many small investors in the stock markets of our own industrial economy.

I should like to pause to give a moment's consideration to those typical companies of the Middle Ages whose activities were at one and the same time industrial, financial, and commercial. Werner Sombart, as usual, has seen in this plurality of functions, or confusion of functions, according to him, a confirmation of the narrow artisan mentality that pervaded the general economy of the time. I think, on the contrary, that this multiplicity of operations, not in the least chaotic in its totality, was undertaken expressly for certain precise objectives, which were indeed achieved. These merchants were attempting, by avoiding the expense of intermediaries and the services of outsiders, to make their enterprises more active, in order to gain more profits. And it was precisely towards this end that the manufacturer who traded in his own products participated also in the activities of the bank which put the necessary funds at his disposal and developed, either by himself or with his partners, all the branches necessary to his enterprise. In principle, each craft guild, each merchant guild, imposed on its members the exercise of a single trade or a single profession. In actual fact, the rule was modified from top to

bottom by the possibility left open to each individual to inscribe himself on the rolls of several guilds. One was only
held, and strictly held, to observe for each branch of activity the statutory rules of the respective guild, to submit
himself to the control of its officers and to the jurisdiction
of its magistrates. Therefore, the great merchant, far from
being irrational, gives us proof of his rationality: by divid-
ing his risks, by not putting all his capital in trade, but putting some in movable goods, some in rural properties, and
some in loans which today we would call government
bonds.

I have already said that the company was made up of
men who knew one another. I shall be more precise and say
that at the beginning, in the early Middle Ages, these men
belonged to the same family, which formed a closed block
of interests and individuals. They lived under the same
roof, submitted to the authority of the eldest among them,
and broke bread around the same table. Like the family, a
compact group by reason of its ties of blood, the company
had its honor to safeguard in society. And this family-com-
pany identity imposed on each of its members a line of irre-
proachable conduct in business affairs. Anyone who com-
mitted a fraud would ruin both his own name and that of
his entire family. This name would be dragged in the mud
also by anyone who deserted the battlefield, made treaties
with the enemy, or broke a sworn peace or a promise of
marriage. In this way there was a rigorous reciprocal control, which was made bearable by the affection uniting the
families.

As the business grew, it required more capital, and
therefore outsiders, capable of supplying the necessary
funds, had to be admitted. These men were chosen from a

wide circle of relatives and associates and finally people who had no particular ties to the family group. Sometimes, however, old associates detached themselves and formed their own companies or joined other combinations. This was indicative of the cult of individualism which began to rise even in these solid family groups and which paved the way for the development of the Renaissance.

Soon, however, a new phase began, although it was not apparent. But perhaps the merchants made an effort to show nothing. Old social values were maintained; the name of the house remained unchanged. A descendant of the founders was left in control even when the founding family had sunk to the second rank in number of partners or volume of capital invested. Moreover, this was all very honest and efficient; the situation of third parties in their relations with the companies underwent no change. If the statutes did not make a legal determination of this new situation, the tribunals accepted the *usus mercatorium*, according to which the companies assumed an unlimited and indivisible responsibility for risks, as had always been the rule.

There was only one occasion at the end of the thirteenth century when there was an attempt to modify the *usus mercatorium* and this was in Siena during the disorder which preceded the failure of the Bonsignori company. The old partners, defending their honor, were opposed by the new adherents, who demanded and obtained from the commune the abolition of the principle of solidarity while maintaining the unlimited liability of the company. As I have shown elsewhere, the petition was accepted, but not without dramatic opposition. The force of custom was such, however, that soon afterwards there was a reversion to former practices. But it was already too late; after the proclamation of the *Constituto* in 1310, businessmen turned away from Siena, preferring the companies of other cities, notably Florence. When Siena became aware of its mistake, it took up again and recodified the practices of the glorious thirteenth century, but markets and clients had been irremediably lost.

These reflections on the responsibility and the honor of the companies lead me to touch upon a basic point: the confidence they had enjoyed carried them away, so that they ended by abusing it. Indeed, even from this point of view, a progressive modification was taking place in their internal organization.

In the beginning "participation" (partnership) had been the instrument that allowed capital to be amassed; later this means was replaced by the deposit. In the beginning the "participant" (partner) had to have unlimited confidence in these early partnerships and had to rely completely on those to whom he had entrusted his capital, without requiring any guarantees. Great vigilance and caution were exercised in the limited negotiations, and the companies had not yet embarked on the dangerous speculations which were to make them lose everything. At that early time, given the restricted nature of the firm, those who had capital at their disposal found more advantages in partnership (which gave them the double remuneration of interest and profits, modest though they were) than in the deposit, which brought them only interest. Since the companies did not have to undergo the bother that the accounting was to cause them later, they used the money from shares with greater freedom than that from deposits. They could have the use of the former over longer periods of time. In the long run, however, when mistrust began to arise among the more numerous and heterogeneous partners about the greater risks being taken, the partner felt the need for protecting himself with the aid of the rights that the law accorded him. The companies, already forewarned by the frequent requests, soon came to realize the inconvenience of such a situation. Outside partners could gain access to the secrets of their management, if only through copies of contracts or account books.

In this second phase the system of partnership was therefore replaced by the deposit. I think I have found an example (and it would be worth the effort of searching for others) in the Sienese statutes, where the rules regulating deposits (*accomandigia*) become more and more numerous as one approaches the fourteenth century; so that, in the *Constituto* of 1310 we find a real novelty: the obligation imposed on the companies to maintain a sufficient reserve of capital, which served as a security fund for the Councils of the *Mercanzia* and a guarantee for the depositors. It is quite justifiable therefore to maintain that the increasing legislative prescriptions on this subject bear a correlation to the growing practice of accepting deposits. The last intervention in Siena took place, in fact, at the time of the failure of the largest Sienese company, which was, moreover, essentially a banking company. After this crash, which affected a large number of depositors, mistrust on the part of the public caused such a lack of deposit money that a freeze in the commercial activity of the city took place. The legislators turned to various expedients to reestablish the indispensable flow of funds, the principal ones being the regulations on the subject of reserves and guarantees that I have just mentioned. And in another domain, by their ratification of the liability of the companies, the legislators tried to reduce the number of partnerships. This same spirit presided at the drawing up of the *Constituto* of 1310.

If it is easy to trace the passage from shareholding to deposits, it is not easy to fix precise dates or to generalize for the whole peninsula, for there was no synchronization between the economic variations of the Italian republics of the thirteenth and fourteenth centuries. In any case, I believe that the middle of the thirteenth century can be considered as the surest demarcation. So, in the beginning, the commercial companies everywhere had the characteristics of our financial companies and stayed like that while they operated alone or mainly with the capital of partners. They became like banking houses or credit establishments in structure when they had used not only capital accumulated through shares, but especially money deposited with them by third parties.

I emphasized the credit and the instrument which is far from being characteristic of craft economy presented by Werner Sombart, but much closer to a capitalist economy. To create this credit, the moral element, which was already included in the *honor familiaris* and transferred later in a rather diffuse way into the *honor societatis*, was not enough. Other circumstances were necessary, which directs our attention, as it surely did that of the men of the thirteenth and fourteenth centuries, to the personalities of the partners. The mention of the *Magna Tavola* of the Bonsignori in the thirteenth century and of the Florentine houses of the Bardi and the Peruzzi in the first half of the fourteenth century recalls legendary images to our minds. We can see the splendor of the courts, in which these merchants were treated with the deference due to persons whom the princes endowed with "the crown," the symbol

of their royalty. The princes renounced the royal preroga-
tive of tax collecting in their favor and even abandoned
their political fortunes to them. We see, too, the magnifi-
cence of the town houses built by these merchants, houses
where they led princely lives in contrast to the very modest
way of life of most people of that period. Since there were
no public buildings as luxurious as these, hospitality was offered to the sovereigns and their brilliant trains of courtiers
in these houses. Also, in the shops on the ground floors of
these palaces, there was a constant flow of people from
every country and of courtiers bringing news of the most
remote regions. We can imagine the capacity of the
guarded strongboxes, resplendent with the gold of all
known currencies. Outside the city walls, in the secluded
countryside, the *case da signore* ("country villas"), built in
the midst of luxuriant vineyards and olive groves, displayed
the armorial bearings of the merchant families. The poor
and modest homes of the workers testified that a small
army worked to contribute to the happiness of the great
and the wealthy. We can imagine other sights, too. The
grave-faced merchants dressed in their *paludamentum* in
the austere rooms of the town hall. Their purses put aside,
their hunting falcons forgotten for the moment, they made
treaties with Popes, the Princes of Anjou, and the Kings of
France, while their horses were tied to the hitching rings
outside. Here they engineered banishments, granted amnes-
ties, received the supplications of the humble, and could an-
ticipate that proud sentence from a future century:
"L'État, c'est nous."

This was a splendid sight, which excites our admiration,
but which hid all too easily the weakness at the base of the
proud edifice. Like the Colossus' feet of clay, the foundations on which this structure rested gave way as too many

heavy and elaborate new constructions were added. If those looking on had seen even for an instant the merest crack in the interior of this edifice, the miracle would have vanished at once, perhaps as unjustly as it had been constructed. But the realization always came too late, at the moment of settlements and catastrophes, at the moment of outcries, of rage, of fraud, only an instant after the enthusiasm of the happy days. The chronicles are full of these dramatic reversals.

The continued growth of business depended on the opening of subsidiary branches in the most important centers. One can get a good idea from the Florentine company of the Bardi, which had permanent representatives with warehouses and offices in Italy at Ancona, Aquila, Bari, Barletta, Castello di Castro, Genoa, Naples, Orvieto, Palermo, Pisa, and Venice; and abroad at Avignon, Barcelona, Bruges, Cyprus, Constantinople, Jerusalem, London, Majorca, Marseilles, Nice, Paris, Rhodes, Seville, and Tunis. The branches were run by partners or by senior employees whose freedom of action was limited by powers of attorney. These branches received instructions from the central management frequently and in some areas at regular intervals. Each branch sent out representatives who did business in the neighboring regions and who depended on instructions from the branches. Such was the recognized importance of the Italian companies abroad that several times their chiefs obtained from the sovereigns, for their city, what we would call today a "most favored nation" clause, and even sometimes obtained this for their own organization, which then enjoyed an exceptional advantage. A typical example is the treaty signed in the early years of the fourteenth century between a director of the Bardi company, Francesco, son of Balduccio Pegolotti, and the King of Armenia.

The realization of these plans required a large specialist personnel in the different branches of mercantile activity. From one of the few books of the Bardi house which have come down to us, we know that the number of employees hired by them in the years between 1310 and 1345 was 346. . . .

For the same reason they needed a whole hierarchy of employees, from office boys to general managers; they also needed departments for correspondence, accounting, and legal advice, consisting of notaries who were salaried, and who, when there were no lawyers, took on various legal functions: some drew up legal papers, while some represented the company in court cases. The contract of employment was favorable to the employees, but the subordinate employees had very little recourse if they happened to be arbitrarily dismissed under pretext of illness, unsatisfactory performance, or reasons of morality.

In this amassing of capital destined for international commerce, what was the role of the different social classes? As to the *commende*, the protocolli of the Genoese notaries show us that the whole population took part, from the nobles on down to the various categories of the bourgeoisie. For the companies, we shall investigate the role of the noble classes. According to our information, the nobility, which at the start had played such a large part in the formation of the commune, was little by little excluded from the control of the republic, with some exceptions, as in Venice. We can then roughly suppose that its economic role was also reduced. Now, this is not very exact. The typical case of Florence bears this out, where there were companies in which the partners were magnates, the Bardi, for example, and also those whose partners were "of the people," as in the case of the Peruzzi. When the economic policies of the city administration had to be discussed at the Palazzo Vecchio, the voice of the leading Peruzzi was raised in agreement with his colleague Bardi, defending their common interests. . . .

However, it is true that in the south, from Rome on down, the nobility kept aloof from business, which was considered to be degrading. In fact, the economy of the southern regions never achieved the same vigor as that of northern and central Italy. This great fact is the origin of the painful question of the Mezzogiorno, which still awaits a solution today.

2. *Means of Communication*

Let us now turn to the means of communication. The state of the roads was naturally very important for the caravans. The medieval traders, conscious of the importance of this problem, mobilized the force of the guilds and the resources of the state to open up, maintain, and make safe those routes needed for the cheapest and quickest transport of merchandise. In this way new passes were found over mountains and through forests, and wars were fought to gain a point of entry for one important market or another.

Along these routes (where the hostels established by the Church to ease the journeys of pilgrims were little by little falling into decay as the commune took over the maintenance and the policing functions and the guilds built "stations" or hostels) the traders organized a courier service for the post, which became fairly regular when the fairs were established in Champagne. A daily courier service to these fairs carried correspondence for the companies and the merchant-bankers. In the early years of the fourteenth century, when these fairs had already gone into decline, the messengers of the Republic of Venice took seven days to reach Bruges. Other itineraries were run by the different companies. The Sienese *Constituti*, the Florentine statutes of the Calimala guild, the Venetian capitularies, all carried provisions on the subject of the couriers. The handbooks on commerce instruct us rather well on these practices— the ethics of the postal service, so to speak—reference to which is also to be found in the treatises of the moralists of the time, who suggest to the company office boy that he should deliver first the letters addressed to the director of the company and then make the general distribution on the following day. Paolo, the son of Pace de Certaldo, writes about the subject: "If you are in business, and with the correspondence of your house they bring you also letters for others, always take care to read your letters first before distributing the other letters; and if your letters suggest your buying or selling certain merchandise for profit, send for a messenger at once and do what your letters propose; only then should you distribute the other letters that arrived with yours, but not before having taken care of your own affairs, because those letters may contain orders which would damage your operations. The service rendered to a friend or a neighbor or to a stranger in delivering his letters might do you a great injury, and you should not serve others to the detriment of yourself and your affairs."

Coastal trade demanded no particular surveillance. But for voyages across the open sea the communes organized escort services of armed galleys. This gave rise to the system called the *mude*, which brought together a large number of ships at dates planned in advance. These "convoys," carrying large quantities of merchandise, facilitated trade enormously. At the ports of arrival when the ships were expected, both buyers and sellers gathered with goods for the return trip, for which similar precautions were taken.

Commerce on the navigable rivers was likewise under regular surveillance. We know the importance of the River Po in the economy of northern Italy. And we have numerous details on river navigation, which was very important for the countries in the center of Europe. The overland routes, especially across the Alps, were costly and were therefore routes for luxury goods. That is why the international traders so often had recourse to the less onerous maritime routes, which were generally faster. Furthermore, on the sea the merchant was not burdened by the payment of the numerous taxes which were exacted on the overland routes every time the goods left one state for another, passed from one city to another, or even crossed a simple bridge. In preference to the land routes, the merchant also used the rivers and the canals expressly dug to link the great watercourses. To meet the needs of water-borne trade, innumerable types of ships were constructed: ships sailed or rowed; deep, long, galleys; barges; skiffs; *marcigliane;* or brigantines. Among these ships, some large carriers stand out. According to recent studies, notably those of Mr. Byrd, several were of greater tonnage than the famous ship *Paradisus Magnus*, which had been considered the largest, and which, in 1251, manned by eighty sailors and twenty crossbowmen, transported from Genoa to Tunis one hundred pilgrims and 80,000 cantars of merchandise (the equivalent of 240 tons). These ships were large, and according to a recent review by Mme. Dohaerd, the Genoese used the same types of ships when they reached the English and Flemish coasts in 1295 after braving the Atlantic. A Mediterranean victory! To the many factors that contributed to the decline of the fairs of Champagne we must add the advantageous prices of the eastern merchants, who began to reach the Flemish markets in great numbers by the sea routes.

It is inconceivable that they would have gone to such trouble for as insignificant a trade as Werner Sombart has made it out to be. In addition to the logical assumption, we have some statistical evidence. It has been shown that the figures given by Villani for the three years 1335 through 1339 were not imagined: 10,000 bales of cloth having a value of 360,000 gold florins were indeed imported annually in those years by the Calimala guild and 70 to 80,000 bales of cloth, worth 1,200,000 gold florins were woven by two hundred wool shops. Most of these textiles were destined for export after being dyed and finished in the Florentine workshops; the smaller number remaining were absorbed by the local market. Surer still are the figures furnished by Bigwood on the export of wool from England, which about the year 1300 attained a yearly figure of 40,-000 sacks, of which 32,743 were exported under regular licenses, the rest as contraband. Forty thousand sacks—that is to say, about 6640 to 8000 metric tons (6640 according to Schaube's calculation of the weight of a sack as 160 kg., 8000 according to Sombart's calculation of 200 kg as the weight of one sack). This amount, not negligible in itself, represents only a part, albeit the greater part, of the wool circulating in Europe for the requirement of its industries. We know that merchants and merchant companies from different countries frequented Spain or had offices there and that one of their foremost aims was to get a corner on the market for the wool of the merino sheep, that wool of high quality which was to have such a brilliant future. We know that the merchants had recourse to the African and Albanian wool markets; that in 1338 Como undertook by treaty to supply the territory of Venice with 12,000 pieces of unfinished cloth yearly, for which the raw material could surely not have been of the same quality as English or Spanish wool. Indeed, we should not forget these second-class wools or the very numerous local markets. The cities which depended most heavily on England, like those in Flanders, themselves produced a significant quantity of wool, and the Abbey of Clairmorais alone possessed a herd of sheep of over 1400 head, a fact that explains the vast dimensions of the export of manufactured products from the Flemish cities, which has been the object of much historical research, especially by Belgian scholars. It is a question of numbers, of volume. In our calculations and reasonings when fixing the proportions between the present day and the medieval world, we should not forget that the demographic factor intervenes and affects all our figures. I would invite those who like to make Sombart-like comparisons to remember the population factor; it must be considered, in addition to the figures, in any estimation of the wool or textile business. I shall, however, make only a passing allusion to this important problem.

I have already mentioned the advantages of the fast transportation. Instead of referring to the days of marching or of sea travel as proof of this assertion, I shall establish a significant comparison on the basis of the work of a French historian, Yves Renouard. In 1336 when Pope Benedict XII wanted to supply wheat to the Armenians, who, overcome by their sufferings and their hunger, were about to submit to the Infidels and abjure their religion, the papal chancellery took weeks merely to transmit the order to the Bardi company, which had been entrusted with the operation. By contrast, the Avignon branch of this Florentine house, which was given 10,000 florins with which to procure the wheat, succeeded in performing its task very quickly: between 10 April and the end of the month, even before the end of the month, its agents in Naples and Bari had brought respectively 4000 and 2000 *salmas* of wheat—more than the 7000 metric tons expected—and had chartered ships to transport the cargoes. It is only by thinking of the organization of the Church, the greatest economic and political institution of the time, that we can measure the effort and the successful achievement of a handful of men who knew what they wanted. In the same way when the London Peruzzis were hit in 1338 by the military disaster of Edward III in his campaign against France and wanted to get the news to their most distant branches so that proper steps could be taken before their creditors panicked, they fitted out a ship which set sail for Rhodes. It is unnecessary to add that they got what they wanted. The echo of disaster, although it was loud, did not arrive until the swift ship had already breasted the waves of the Channel, the Atlantic, and the Mediterranean.

3. *Conditions in International Trade*

The preceding section prepares for our last question: were luxury goods of great price and small volume the only objects of international trade? Or should we add cheap merchandise, which was both heavy and awkward? Sombart and those who have adhered to his explanation of medieval economy believe that the traffic was limited to the first category, that of costly merchandise. Undoubtedly, the cost of long distance transportation was not negligible, although up to the present time we have had but few facts,

those recently gathered by Carlo Cipolla, to go on. But
these facts, upon which this young historian has exercised
his natural cleverness, are limited, disorganized, and, I
might even say, disconcerting.

According to the old treatises on the history of commerce, all or almost all of the trade in the Middle Ages con-
sisted in the buying and selling of spices. Certainly, large
transactions were carried out in pepper, cinnamon, cloves,
saffron, all widely used in cooking, and in sugar, which was
used also in pharmaceutical preparations. Their importance,
rising out of the great demand, is proved by the simple fact
that the law sometimes allowed, during periods of scarcity
of these products, a debtor to discharge part of his debt by
forcing his creditors to accept one of these products, more
precisely, pepper, in partial payment. The law in effect
gave pepper the same freedom as money. We can get a
more exact idea of the importance of spices in international
trade when we understand the importance of the dyes and
tints included under this heading: alum, cochineal, purple,
madder, indigo, brazil, guago, etc., and when we consider
their uses in the textile industry which was basic to the
economy of the times. As the production of these raw materials was confined to certain specific regions, especially
the East, and as they were used throughout the West, they
were transported in great quantities to Europe. Salt, which
was cheaper than pepper, was also greatly sought after and
was also heavily taxed. Hence the attempts of the princes
to gain a monopoly, and the imperialistic politics of certain
states. For example, Venice not only exploited its own salt
marshes but got a monopoly on the production of neighboring territories. An increase in the demand for salt followed naturally from the use of salted meat by travelers on
sea and on land and still more from the use of salt fish,

which was consumed in great quantities as a consequence of the scrupulous observance of the precepts of the Church during fast days. For this reason quantities of salt were shipped from the Adriatic, whose waters were very salty, to the North Sea ports, where the Hanseatic peoples, and later the Frisians and the English, harvested their teeming waters, which were relatively fresh. But the seas, and especially the seas of southern Europe, could not supply the enormous demand. The Vitti of Scandinavia got their supplies near at hand, from places where salt was extracted from springs or mines. There were salt works at Salins in Burgundy, at Luneburg in Germany, at Cracow and Lvov in Poland, and at Droitwich in England. . . . The salt mines of the Tyrol supplied the Danubian basin as far as Bohemia by the Linz-Freistadt route, which was justly called "the iron and salt route." Nevertheless, throughout the whole of the Middle Ages another method was also used for preserving fish, and that was smoking it.

Wine was obviously a much-traveled commodity. Naturally the finest wines were preferred. In regions where vines did not flourish, there was no lack of an alcoholic drink among the lower classes, who had recourse to beer or cider. . . . But there was also an active traffic in wines. Cyprian wine traveled as far as London, and, like that of Crete, was consumed in Constantinople and on the shores of the Black Sea, as were the wines of the Crimea and Lower Rumania. French wines, whose diffusion across the Channel at an early date has been pointed out in a classic study by Henri Pirenne, were consumed on the continent as far as Flanders, where they competed with the much appreciated wines of the Moselle and the Rhine. First in Bruges and later on the Adriatic coast the Hanseatic traders bought up these French wines to satisfy the very active demand in the Low Countries. Furthermore, and contrary to the opinion of the Belgian historian, we must not ignore the fact that French wine was also traded at that time in the Mediterranean basin. It was exported even as far as the Holy Land, where, if it was not sought after by the Infidels because of the Koranic prohibition, it was welcomed by the Crusaders. To cite only two cases among many: in 1229, a wineshop owned by merchants from Marseilles prospered in Tunis; in 1291, considerable quantities of French wine were carried as far as the Black Sea.*

Slaves constituted an important item of trade. In spite of the opposition of their respective churches, Christians traded their fellow Christians to the Moslems and the latter sold their brothers into slavery on the continent of Europe. More than once, high dignitaries of the Church, bishops, and archbishops, made a present to their friends of "little slave girls, young and well-formed." The rulers of Egypt created the selected corps of Mamelukes and filled it with young boys especially imported from Dalmatia and Sclavonia.

Other more ordinary commerce: the Moslems were in the market for, and the Italians were the principal providers of, shipments of wood, pitch, and cordage for their "naval armies." These materials were sent to them even in times of crisis, as during the Crusades.

The trade of arms, horses, and minerals was also impor-

---

* We must remember too that the religious tenor of the times increased the demand for oil. If we think of the sumptuous ceremonies in the churches and the fact that in the wills of the nobles and of all people of means there was specified perpetual illumination for the altars and a brighter illumination during the numerous masses that were celebrated for the safety of their souls, we have an idea of the amount of oil that was burned in the Middle Ages. And oil was also less expensive than wax, which was produced mostly in the Moslem countries.

tant. I should also like to emphasize the importance of the circulation of gold as merchandise. On this subject a vast horizon has been opened by the studies of Marc Bloch, a pioneer of learning and a martyr to liberty, and also by his students and friends, especially Maurice Lombard. The last point I want to make is about the transport of wheat, which was extremely important. Documents show that there was a steady market for this, and therefore one cannot deny that bulky goods were carried over long distances.

It was soon realized that food would have to be provided for a constantly increasing population, and so woods were cleared and land reclaimed. Indubitably, as the land became freed from the feudal system (because of the formation of communes in Italy and because the lords needed ready cash in other countries), it passed over to a new class of landowners, more interested in public affairs, which increased the cultivation of grain. At the same time, the towns were growing, together with the number of artisans, and strong external competition demanded a marked self-sufficiency in food. However, for geographic reasons in the cases of Syria, Egypt, Libya, Tunisia, and Scandinavia, or for demographic reasons in the case of Constantinople, the Po valley including Venice, and the Brabant, certain regions could not always support themselves. To meet the task of supplying these areas of high consumption, three great breadbaskets took form little by little: the countries bordering on the North Sea, Prussia, and Sicily and Apulia, to which we can add Sardinia, but to a lesser degree. We can guess their power and attraction; why the princes tried to obtain control monopolies there, as in the case of salt. The wheat trade is at the bottom of much of the politics of the medieval princes. Frederick II, for example, strengthened his ties with Egypt for these reasons, and Charles of Anjou made use of his title of King of Jerusalem to speculate on the hunger of the Crusaders. Certainly they controlled the movement of wheat with taxes which helped to restore their finances. It was not for nothing that speculators asked for the right to move the wheat and paid heavily for these privileges. Sometimes they would even fight for them. The attraction of wheat was such that Florentine and Venetian speculators often asked for the right to export it and consented to make large and risky advances to the royal treasuries in exchange for this privilege. On such occasions, furious struggles took place among the competing merchants. For similar reasons the popes bought up great quantities of wheat at pre-established prices, with the permission or complaisance of their protégés and protectors, the House of Anjou.

In the north, thanks to the Hanseatic traders, Prussian wheat often nourished the Brabant and its neighbors and sometimes even England, which during the Black Death had to seek its food supply from continental sources.

In the same way Venice (whose treaties are extant, notably the pact with Ravenna by which Venice prevented that city from exporting wheat even to its neighbors Bologna, Faenza, and Ferrara) was the supplier of wheat to all the valley of the Po and even beyond the Apennines. Neapolitan nobles established warehouses in Palestine, where wheat could be preserved for long periods of time, and thus wheat from their lands was collected there and sold in Corfu, in Egypt, in Tunis, in Bône, and in Bougie. Constantinople was a vast center for the consumption, transit, and re-export of wheat, as we can see from the *consigli* of Pegolotti to the speculators who bought up wheat there to sell elsewhere. Constantinople found itself in trouble when shipments were slowed down because of a bad harvest or transportation difficulties, or when the Italian merchants tried to exercise powerful political pressures by threatening the city with famine or by actually provoking one. In the valuable study made by De Bouard, which should be extended, it is established that, apart from the inevitable contraband, the official export of wheat from Sicily between 1268 and 1282 was 645,000 salmas, while local consumption on the island was 6,000 salmas.

I personally agree with the line of thought presented by Carlo Cipolla, who states that if wheat was included in the circuit of international commerce in the Middle Ages, it was because it was needed by the countries which had poor supplies of wheat. Naturally, economic advantages and profits must not be excluded from our considerations. But necessity was a compelling force, and this is why the food relief policies of these states was so complicated and vigilant and also so instructive to the student of history. Hunger made them look for all sources of wheat. It made them invent the "shipping policies" which were in operation during the many famines. In 1363 Venice restricted the transport of wheat from the east to ships of over 265 tons in an effort to encourage imports. Speculation had to be restricted and Gino Luzatto has described very competently the attempts to create cartels and trusts in Venice. At this point I shall unfortunately have to stop my trip on this most fascinating road through history.

Chapter Three

THE ITALIANS
ABROAD

M EDIEVAL HISTORIOGRAPHY seems to have reached a stopping point in 1922 with the publication of the second edition of Werner Sombart's *Der moderne Kapitalismus.* Received with marked favor by the devotees of the fashionable, who have representatives even in the domain of science, this work was criticized severely by the enemies of progress, those individuals whose mental torpor is threatened by every innovation. It gave rise to fierce polemics from the opposing camps. Werner Sombart, who had received the praises with indifference, answered the attacks fiercely. Such behavior is useless and can sometimes cause pain. Now that calm has been restored we can, on deeper examination, put into evidence the imperfections, voluntary or involuntary, of Sombart's work. Of these imperfections, the first concerns the construction as a whole, which seeks to distinguish the essence (*das Wesen*) of the Middle Ages by means of the pretended uniformity of its aspects in all the countries of Europe. This gave no weight to the variety of situations that prevailed during a period which, from the political point of view, had known both small communes and great unified states. From the civil point of view, whether it be a social, juridical, or artistic aspect, a profound difference was manifested between regions which had experienced the influence of Rome in very different ways. From the economic point of view, objective possibilities and impossibilities of development had been revealed, corresponding to the cultural conditions I have just mentioned. In the Middle Ages the factor of geography could not help but exercise its particularly important function of differentiation.

Werner Sombart himself constructed his medieval uniformity by orienting himself in the milieu of German *Kultur* and by taking as a symbol of a whole world and a whole epoch the political appearance of the largest of the structures of that epoch, the Holy Roman Empire.

Now this political structure, far from reproducing the values of the colossus whose name it had borrowed with a slight modification, embraced those vast territories only nominally. It was of decisive importance only in the interior of central Europe. From the heart of this massive structure, it was inevitable that the little states (including the Italian communes) should seem to live in the shade; that the plains of Champagne should appear extremely flat when viewed from those high altitudes; that the maritime countries should disappear into thin air, and that the little ships which plied the Mediterranean should appear on the horizon as imperceptible pinpoints often shrouded by fog.

And yet what a prodigious life animated these maritime towns and their hinterlands in Flanders, on the southern coast of France, and Italy! And what destinies pushed the ships far out to sea, to shuttle between the banks of two continents! These adventurous ships were laden with men-at-arms destined to battle pirates and with merchandise destined to establish, to renew, and then to intensify the exchanges between the East and the West. These ships were sailed by men for whom the voyages were not simply military enterprises or commercial ventures, but the opportunity, eagerly sought after, to know other men and other political situations, other institutions and other mentalities, let us even say to participate in the scientific thought, spontaneous or reflective, of all the cultures they touched on. And let us add that these voyages took place precisely at the moment when the center of Europe was awaiting the signal for awakening and renewal from the merchants of the little city-states: "Venice, the greatest lesson in energy and will in history," said Renan in a cry of heartfelt admiration.

Let us return to Werner Sombart: when he deliberately set himself on the road we have just described, when he surveyed all the body of history which was the object of his studies, he chose to consider those phenomena which were in accord with what he had studied most carefully and to neglect those which he regarded, from his own fixed and rigid position, merely as occasional deviations of the sort that confirm the rule. His rule was this: the Middle Ages, the entire European Middle Ages, were dominated by the mentality and the spirit of the artisan, and the formation of its wealth—first in the form of inheritance, later in the form of capital—was founded everywhere on revenues from the land. This is equivalent to mounting an attack on the fundamental principle of historical investigation, which tries, by tracing the strands of causality, to find the links between the great periods and to account for sudden spurts of progress or abrupt reversals, the one as un-expected as the other.

In other words, Sombart did not find the link that unites the civilization of the Middle Ages with that of the Renaissance and modern times. He did not find it because, in the history of Germany in the fifteenth century its in-distinct outline is difficult to identify, even though it ap-peared in a developed form and was very evident in the his-tory of other countries, notably in the history of Italy.

1. The Two Aspects of the Medieval World

In reality, one can notice a great diversity of situation between continental Europe and maritime Europe, even during the early centuries but particularly from the tenth century on. But this is not all. Even in those areas which were most advanced in all aspects of civilization—and let us not forget the importance of the economic aspect—we no-tice the coexistence of two worlds. On the one hand, the traditional world, and consequently, an essentially medieval world, with its typical organization into crafts, on which the writings of Alfred Dopsch are fundamental regarding Italy. It is the world of masters and apprentices, of innu-merable workshops where a humble crowd of artisans, usually unlettered and uncultivated, produced for a market restricted to the limits of one city or one quarter, using as a medium of exchange the coins of the *piccoli*. It is a world in which the authority of the Church and government by the statutes of the communes and the guilds held sway without restraint, a world in which the intimate satisfaction of doing artisan-like work, and sometimes of creating a masterpiece, substituted for the satisfaction of material well-being.

In addition to this, there was also the world of the avant-garde, consisting of companies dealing with international trade and of rich warehouses piled high with costly goods, where sophisticated and cultured men with long experience, bold views, and unbounded ambition conducted commercial and financial dealings with the main economic centers abroad and handled not only the golden florins but the moneys of all the other countries.

These two worlds were both organized on the twofold base of the moral laws of the Church and the statutory laws of the city and the guilds. It is not surprising therefore that scholars who have consulted only the statutes should have formed an idea of, and acquired an understanding of, only one world—that of the guilds. However, while these statutes remained really binding on the artisans, so that they stifled all budding initiative and kept all modes of life and all activity on the same level, for the great merchants they had a value more formal than substantial. Established in the final analysis by those men who played a preponderant role in the politics of the communes and the economy of the guilds, in spite of the complicated mechanism of decisions taken by vote or by drawing lots, these laws represented for the favored few merely a providential screen behind which they could take measures that led them without risk toward their own ends. And if they happened to meet an obstacle in one of the laws that they themselves had so skillfully drawn up, and if it was finally impossible to disguise or to justify a violation, they overcame the obstacle with as much audacity as savoir faire, which, however, is not a proceeding which is unique to the Middle Ages. . . . But if one interprets the statutory law literally, and if one thinks that all men were equal before it, one can never explain the formation of fabulous wealth, of monopolies and trusts, or of that economic organization which has no reason to envy the later one that historians and economists have called by common accord "the organization of capital."

In spite of its functional importance, the world of the artisan was destined to decline and find itself on the downward path throughout historical process. And this is because the very reasons for its existence and its long persistence became progressively less compelling. By contrast, given the new situations, the world of the merchant-bankers was destined to put down deep roots, which would assure it a flowering of future prosperity. Prosperity, I repeat, that one cannot understand nor justify historically without linking it to the past in all its roots. The Renaissance is not a period of splendid light which suddenly exploded after unheard-of mortifications inflicted on God's creatures and on their intelligence. On the contrary, it is the result of a logical evolution that took place when the growing frontiers of the known world, the technical progress in certain sectors, and the diffusion of knowledge and of cultural interests had all contributed to allow more and more groups to participate in a way of life and in aspirations which up until then had belonged to a minority of the privileged. The situation underwent a gradual reversal: while we see emerging into the limelight those forces that had been shrouded in darkness because they had escaped the incomplete visual field of the historians, we see, on the other hand, those forces which had formerly occupied the foreground, by reason of the weight of their numbers and their robust juridical and social organization, retreating into silence and oblivion, without, however, disappearing altogether.

And now I propose to sketch the outlines of the second aspect of what I have called the double existence of the

Middle Ages. I propose to evoke some living vignettes of this faraway world, vignettes that Sombart has insufficiently studied, when he has not totally neglected them. I shall speak, in a word, of the Italians in the world.

2. The Arab Invasions and Italy

The Italians in the world! For this supreme adventure they had long prepared themselves—as do all who aspire to difficult conquests—by means of a harsh discipline that tempers energies and selects individuals. At the time of the Arab invasions, the cities of the Tyrrhenian coast, Genoa, and especially Pisa, learned how to prepare themselves for war as they built up heavy defenses while waiting for attacks. Thus it came about that the Arabs, who had hitherto known the intoxication of pillage and the destruction of foreign territory, had to undergo the sad experience of seeing the pillage and destruction of their own homeland, which was ravaged as far as Media. But here and there, a sense of business survived in the face of martial spirit, and this was regarded as a sign of irresponsibility by the prejudiced. When they met each other during the truces, Italians and Mohammedans violated the precepts of their respective religions, a sign of a lack of principles, but also a proof of vitality. Because of this, the contacts and collisions that put these two peoples in the presence of each other were not as sterile as the consequences of warfare alone would have been. It was thanks to something other than a pure spirit of battle that the Italians, on the one hand, prepared themselves unconsciously for the economic role they were to play during the Crusades, and that the Arabs, on the other hand, left a deep imprint on the countries where they lived the longest, that is to say, Sicily and Spain. In their passage, both the one and the other cut a furrow that the sword could not have made as deep or as lasting.

Under the shelter of the Arab incursions, our maritime cities along the Adriatic coast above the narrow gate of the straits of Otranto underwent a prodigious surge of prosperity. Venice managed to free itself from Byzantium, to chase the pirates from the sea, and to extend its prestige and its commercial and political hegemony over both coasts of the Mediterranean; Amalfi, Bari, and Trani formed multiple ties with the countries of the opposite shore, from Egypt to Jerusalem, thus anticipating the commercial regime which was to affirm itself later in the center and in the north of the peninsula and to disappear in the south under the Normans. It should be noted that while Amalfi, Bari, and Trani conducted trade in the lands from Egypt to Jerusalem they laid the groundwork for future Italian business establishments in the Holy Land at the time of the Crusades.

3. The Crusades and the Italians

With the start of the Crusades, the Mediterranean played an important part in shaping the course of events, more clearly perhaps than in the days of Ancient Rome when navigation had been almost exclusively monopolized by other nationalities. This time it depended entirely on the sailors, ships, and merchants of the Italian republics.

It would be superfluous to insist on the importance of the Crusades, since there are most competent research collections in existence which have been compiled by French scholars. But I hope I may be permitted to call attention in passing to an aspect of this important phenomenon that especially concerns Italy and which French historians have not had occasion to study closely. I refer to the military effort of the Italians. Although not comparable to that of the Franks, it represents a real contribution which must be taken into account in making an exact evaluation, in the light of a total historical vision, of the quantities of material and the numbers of soldiers employed in those distant enterprises.

It is certainly not my intention to extol the military glories, those important factors in history that I fervently hope will not figure in the future among its determining elements. Nevertheless, I cannot state without some bitterness that, in one of the most solemn adventures in history, the Italian should habitually appear only in the guise of a greedy and grasping merchant. Now I should like to make it clear that all the skill, intelligence, and moral independence of these adventurous men is not enough to explain fully the success they attained in the economic field. To these qualities there must be added another that cannot be neglected without doing injustice to the factual truth. And this is to be found in the blood they shed for an ideal.

4. Italian Expansion Abroad

As the volume of traffic across the Mediterranean increased, and when, for this reason, the fairs of Champagne attained their highest development, the Italians too had their task and their role to play, which Sombart seems to have almost totally ignored.

I should like to draw some parallels between these celebrated fairs and the ancient Greek Olympic games. The elements are different: the concrete character of the economic exchanges at the fairs, as against the ideal and moral values of the athletic contests and the nobility of the religious celebration; but in both cases there were unforeseen results which were real and considerable. The Olympics gave to Greece a sense of unity that was otherwise beyond the reach of the political polychromy of the city-states. Similarly, at the fairs of Champagne a European mentality was formed, a mentality that had already been foreshadowed in the coming together of the knights of the Cross.

In the foreground of the Olympics was the contest, where young athletes with well-formed bodies vied for prizes in beauty, agility, and suppleness; where the laurel crowns were garnered by poets and writers who spoke in different dialects, but nevertheless in a common language. During these celebrations, a host of problems concerning the transport of multitudes, their lodgings, and their food had to be resolved.

In the foreground at the fairs of Champagne, on the contrary, the direct goal was economic. But on the fringes of this vast market, which resembled an enormous crossroads, there was a mingling of languages and ideas and the organization of brilliant fêtes. It was the remarkable work of France's own M. Huvelin which enlightened me as to the exact importance of these fairs. In the framework of European universality, they contributed greatly to the diffusion and development of economic institutions. Now in this double field of action, the Italians played an extremely important role with the help of their technical skills, their currency, and their civilization, which was already illumined by a renascent art, was ready, through the medium of the same language used by the merchants, to create Dante's masterpiece.

At the beginning of the thirteenth century the conditions that were to produce the systematic penetration of

Italians into all the countries of the known world were already present, and several isolated cases had already appeared by the tenth century. By the first half of the twelfth century some Italians had settled in Ypres, where the Count of Flanders, Charles the Good, bought from these merchants *ex longobardorum regno* a precious vase for which he paid twenty silver marks. Also at Ypres Pope Innocent III ordered the payment of a debt of 1150 marks contracted by Bishop Theodoric of Utrecht with a company comprised of four merchants from Rome and two from Lucca. In Poland, a certain Laurenzio Angelo in 1148 directed the work of extracting iron ore from the mines at Schmiederberg. Among the papers of the notary scribe in Tunis there is a bill of exchange in Arabic ghawâba, dated 1162, that informs us of business dealings between a Genoese and a Moslem. Furthermore, in a contract dated 1157, the sheik of Tunis engaged with the city of Pisa to welcome the Pisans under his protection, not to trade in Pisan prisoners as slaves, and to renounce in their favor the customs duties on merchandise not sold but taken back by sea.

From the thirteenth century on, the ever-increasing Italian emigration took on various aspects as it was favored by this or that circumstance. It did not always have, in the beginning, an exclusively commercial goal. To cite only one example: the Dukes of Anjou, who were at that time masters of Naples, invited a considerable number of their Italian subjects to come to the south of France, particularly to Provence, and gave them positions in the administration of finance and justice. Therefore a crowd of people from all walks of life followed the Anjous to France . . . doctors, notaries, carpenters, wool weavers, apothecaries, goldsmiths. These isolated cases did not, however, constitute the principal strand of Italian emigration over the Alps. I shall try now to give a general outline of this phenomenon.

The Italian businessmen who crossed the frontiers either by sea or by land generally undertook these voyages with the purpose of retrieving the money they had put at the disposition of foreign kings and barons whose expeditions to the Holy Land had been financed by them. These kings and barons had mortgaged their goods and properties as security for their debts. When the Italian merchants went abroad to collect these debts, they usually had occasion to remain a long time. It was often difficult to get cash payment or to take this money across the frontiers of the state where they were doing business. These difficulties gave them the idea of liquidating their rights in the movable and immovable assets of their debtors and of investing the cash received in merchandise to sell either there or elsewhere.

In England, for example, it was recognized on all sides that it was very advantageous to pay the Italian merchant-bankers in woolen goods. These products, very abundant in a country where the economy was based essentially on herding and grazing, were much sought after by Italian industries, which could not find raw materials of comparable quality at home. These industries were often obliged to get the necessary raw materials from Spain or Africa with great difficulty.

These long sojourns abroad and these contacts with the nobility and the clergy led the Italian merchant-bankers to frequent the foreign courts, if only to obtain safe-conducts, residence, travel, or export permits. Another occasion to reside abroad was offered by the popes, who gave them the job of collecting the tithes for the Crusades or the various revenues owed the Church by the princes, ecclesiastic or lay. The sums thus gathered were transferred to Rome or to a named place. The Italian bankers performed the necessary operations not only by transmitting sums of money, but also by addressing orders of payment to their agents who resided in the localities indicated for the reception of the tithes and revenues. A Sienese named Angelerio, treasurer to Gregory IX, was one of the earliest *camsores papae*, as they were then called. Later, in the second half of the thirteenth century, from the reign of Alexander IV until those of Urban IV, Clement IV, Gregory X, and John XXI, the reigning pontiffs could choose their confidential agents from a veritable multitude, for Italians from every city of the peninsula went abroad in greater numbers. Nicholas III (1277–1280) entrusted the receipt of contributions in the Germanic countries to the Frescobaldi and the Alfani of Florence. The latter were also charged with receiving the contributions *in partibus Romanie*, that is to say, the Byzantine Empire. The pope entrusted these same functions for Portugal, Sardinia, and Corsica to the Battosi and the Caccianimici of Lucca; and for England, to the Ricciardi, also from Lucca. Martin IV (1281–1285) distributed the zones of work in the following manner: *Tuscia et partes maritime* to the Bonsignori of Siena; England and Scotland to the Spigliati, the Spini, the Cerchi, the Alberti, the Scali, and the Frescobaldi of Florence; Portugal to the Ammannati of Pistoia and the Cardellini and the Battosi of Lucca; Cologne, Bremen, and Magdeburg to the Spini and the Spigliati, and the other Germanic countries to their Florentine compatriots, the Abbati, the Frescobaldi, and the Alfani; Hungary, Sclavonia, and Poland to the Alfani. In addition, he assigned to the Squarcialupi of Lucca the territory of Greenland and its adjoining regions, where the deniers of the Church were collected not in money but *in bovinis et focarum coriis ac dentibus et funibus balena-*

rum. The fact of being *campsores domini papae* permitted these agents to dispose of considerable sums of money, at least temporarily, which might even be used for their personal affairs, as in the operations of exchange called *valimentum.* The pope's agents also enjoyed the august protection of the Church, a precious advantage in those regions often hostile to, or suspicious of, strangers.

The circumstances that introduced the Italian merchant-bankers into the courts of all these countries gave the sovereigns the idea of attaching these active and intelligent men to their own service. They asked them for loans, gave them the task of handling their disbursements, and made them the directors of the mints. They employed them as official representatives, if not as ambassadors, as at the court of France in the case of the brothers Musciatto and Ciampolo Franzesi, originally from Siena, the famous "Biche" and "Mouche," who were sometimes blamed for having wickedly advised the falsifiers of the currencies about Philippe the Bel's currency and sometimes praised for having vainly proffered good advice that was not heeded. Let us note another personage on the scene around the turn of the thirteenth century: Scaglio Tifi, treasurer to the Dukes of Burgundy and the decisive force in the union of the Duchy of Burgundy to the crown of France. Dino Rapondi was director of a merchant-banking house with offices in Bruges, Paris, Anvers, Avignon, Venice, and in the eastern Mediterranean. In France he supervised the building of military defense works and was a diplomat and a minister for the house of Burgundy, one of whose members he ransomed from the Sultan Bajazet for the sum of 100,000 ducats. In the ducal chapel in Dijon, where he was buried in 1415, there is a statue, a remarkable work of art which reproduces the features of Dino Rapondi, and a long inscription that keeps alive the memory of his complex and meritorious career.

Once, on seeing that the ambassadors of the foreign courts who came to pay him homage were all Florentines, Pope Boniface VIII exclaimed: "These Florentines are truly the fifth element of the universe!"

The activity of the Italians stationed in England sheds light on one of the most characteristic aspects of the role that my compatriots formerly played in foreign lands. In England the Ricciardi family from Lucca and the Florentine families of the Frescobaldi, the Bardi, and the Peruzzi, grouped in a company, succeeded one another as moneylenders to the crown. They ended by having the administration of the state in their hands, and even the fate of kings. Thanks to their loans, the first three Edwards could pursue their policy of trying to conquer Scotland, and Edward III could embrace his dream of extending his sovereignty onto the continent, a policy that provoked the initial phase of the Hundred Years War, in which the Florentine companies who had undertaken all of the expenses of the military expeditions were ruined by the failure of the first campaigns on French soil.

I shall not dwell here on the famous bankruptcy of the Bardi and the Peruzzi in 1345, a most dramatic event that Giovanni Villani related in an unforgettable page of his chronicles. In mentioning the sums owed by the king of England, the Florentine writer added: *che valeano uno reame:* "they were worth a kingdom." The historians have spoken of the bad faith of the king; and from Luigi Simone Peruzzi to Alessandro Luzio, they have calculated exactly what England might be said to owe Italy today: taking the interest into account, the whole British Empire and the islands of the mother country would be necessary to liquidate the ancient debt!

In reality, this credit, annulled by extinctive prescription for lack of claims made in the stipulated time, was the object of a transaction on the part of Richard II, to whom the representatives of the most important company, the Bardi, delivered in 1391 a notarized foreclosure. Nevertheless, what was in no way annulled was the moral value of the event and the documentation of the episode, which shows us that a handful of men, mostly Florentines, held England in their power, as the Anglo-Saxons hold in tutelage our country, now poor—poor because of the inexorable course of events and the errors of men. But it once knew a splendor whose memory, *aere perennius*, is written in indelible letters in the history of civilization.

To try to give an idea of the proportion of Italians emigrating at the end of the thirteenth century, I should like to cite, for a few cities only, the names of families whose members went out in great numbers across the different countries of Europe. With the help of concrete facts we can retrace the voyages of a group of Italians in the Middle Ages.

First, the inhabitants of Asti, who early left their city to cross the mountains: the Alfieri, the Asinari, the Da Saliceto, the Garetti, the Malabaila, the Pelleta, the Roveri, the Scarampi, the Solari, the Toma, to whom also must be added the Provano, originally from Carignano, the Medici di Chieri, and a crowd of Florentines (thirty-seven of whom were counted at the fair of Lagny, in the first half of the fourteenth century). The *registrum lumbardorum* preserved in Fribourg, Switzerland, reveals a veritable invasion of people from Asti in the fourteenth century and contains a complete list of the local nobility whose members, in debt to the Italians for numerous loans, ended by ceding to their creditors their fiefs, their châteaux, and their lands.

From Lucca the Barca, the Burlamacchi, the Calcinelli, the Cenami, the Corbolani, the Forteguerra, the Guinigi, the Onesti, the Ricciardi, the Raponi, the Schiatti, the Spiafame, and the Trenta. Although many of these traders reached England, they mostly settled in France.

The name of Pistoia was known in several countries in Europe, thanks to the companies of the Ammannati, the Cancellari, the Dondori, the Panciatichi, the Partini, and the Simiglianti.

The name of Florence as the triumph of the gold florins show, enjoyed a renown throughout all Europe, wherever there were representatives or agents of the Bardi, the Peruzzi, the Acciaiuoli (whom Villani called "the pillars of Christianity"), the Alberti, the Albizi, the Antellesi, the Ardinghelli, the Baroncelli, the Bondelmonti, the Cerchi, the Del Bene, the Falconieri, the Frescobaldi, the Gianfigliazzi, the Portinari, the Pulci, the Rimbertini, the Scali, the Spini, the Strozzi, et al. . . .

As for Siena, we have a collection of remarkable letters from the thirteenth century, published by Paoli and Piccolomini, from which we learn that towards the middle of that century a number of Sienese companies were established in France, several of them having branches also in Flanders, England, and Germany. In France there were the companies of the Bonsignori, the Cacciaconti, the Fini, the Gallerani, the Maffei, the Marescotti, the Piccolomini, the Sansedoni, the Squarcialupi, the Tolomei, the Ugolini, and the Vincenti. Siena, the great Ghibelline city of Tuscany, reached the height of its political fortunes in the years between 1260—the Battle of Montaperti—and 1268—the Battle of Tagliacozzo. However, the early years of the fourteenth century were still a time of well-being in this city, put to the test but not defeated by the failure of the *Magna Tavola* of the Bonsignori and by the competition of the Florentine capitalists. At the start of the fourteenth century Sienese companies continued to hold their own abroad, like the Cinughi, the Forteguerri, the Malavolti, the Rossi, the Squarcialupi, the Tolomei, and the Salimbeni, who in 1282 had given to Ugo di Ugolini a power of attorney so that he might wind up their affairs in Tuscany, Lombardy, Sicily, France, England, Spain, and Germany.

The list of names I have just cited is rather long, but it is far from being complete. I have limited myself to the most important companies, those best known, composed of families which still exist in our times, and whose memory is linked, in Italy and abroad, with works of art, with military enterprises, and with political events and diplomatic successes.

In order to understand the development of the commercial colonies of an Italian city in those times of long ago, let us imagine we are—along with Roberto Lopez—with those groups of Genoese who in the fourteenth century set out twice a year, in the spring and autumn. After the scribe has registered on the ship's manifesto the names of the passengers and has listed the merchandise—textiles of cotton, wool, and linen, weapons, and sometimes slaves (who are merchandise, too)—the ship lifts anchor and we leave port. Sometimes we skirt the coast of the Italian peninsula as far as Sicily, or else sail in an almost straight line for Corsica and Sardinia, after which starts the crossing of the "great blue sea" towards Bougie or Tunis. From Tunis we make for Tripoli; then, as there is no advantage in stopping on the coast of Cyrenaica, we set sail for Alexandria, that great market where men of all races sell the greatest variety of articles. A new cargo is loaded into the hold, and we may set out for Acre, Tyre, and Antioch, where we take on mostly pilgrims. But more often we steer for Famagusta in Cyprus, for—and it is a German traveler who says it— "there are more spices in Cyprus than bread in Germany." One can always buy something in Famagusta, even though spices have already been taken on at Alexandria. And there will be more spices at our next stop, Latakia, at the crossing of the routes from Syria and Egypt with the route which, traversing Asia Minor, comes out on the Black Sea and, passing by Sivas, leads to Armenia and Persia. "Know," says Marco Polo, "that all the spices and cloths of gold and silk of the country are carried to that city." In addition, cattle from the hinterland are taken to this port; we take on a fair number of the best quality, to be unloaded in Phocaea, on the Turkish coast. At the time we take our journey this ancient Genoese possession—where Benedetto Zaccaria had made his fortune in the thirteenth century exploiting the deposits of alum—this ancient Phocaea is still famous for its mines from which 750 tons of this precious product are extracted each year. Gaining the open sea again, our ship set its course for Chios, "the island of wines," the beautiful island where all the products of the Mediterranean abound and to which ships go especially to find "mastic," used in the distillation of an exquisite liqueur and also in the preparation of a dentifrice.

The next port is Constantinople, that great crossroads of all the commerce of the Levant. Our Genoese band has never been so busy; important and lengthy affairs prolong our stay in the capital city of the Byzantine Empire. Next we go to Kaffa, sailing on a diagonal course, following the coast as far as Vicina, at the mouth of the Danube, to take on textiles and spices, to buy wheat and leather, wax and honey. Many Genoese had settled in Kaffa after 1260, when the Paleologues, favored by Genoa, succeeded to the Latin Empire in the east, whose previous rulers had been supported by Venice. Chased from Kaffa by the Tartars in 1308, the Genoese returned several years later. By 1362 they had solidly fortified the city. A traveler of the time reports that he saw two hundred ships at anchor in this port, where the variety of goods exchanged was unheard of. One could find wheat and furs from Russia, wax, salt fish, and silks from China, which were exchanged for manufactured products, wines, or drugs.

Let us resume our journey. Our sea voyage ends on the opposite shore of the Black Sea, at Sinopus, or Ceresonde, or even at Trebizond at the gates of Persia. Here the Genoese sell the products they have bought in the Crimea and leave their ship. We can push on by land as far as China, across countries about which Marco Polo and, after him, other writers like Francesco Balducci Pegolotti have given us much valuable information. The inhabitants are hospitable, and the routes safe and under rigorous surveillance. But we must interrupt our journey before reaching Cathay; only a rare few went as far as Peking in those days.

Escorted by the Tartar police, after a long and difficult march through the mountains, we reach Sivas. After twelve more days on horseback, or thirty days by caravan, we arrive at Tabriz, the capital of Persia. At the time of our voyage Tabriz is the happy rival of Baghdad in the importance of its market, where one can procure at good prices silks, brocades, muslins, and pearls from the Persian Gulf, and all sorts of spices brought from India and China over the land route across Central Asia, or by sea from Bassorah and Baghdad. From Tabriz we might even push on to the *partes*

Indiae, where in 1315 two of our Genoese compatriots, Benedetto Vivaldi and Perceval Stancone, went to set up in business. But it is time to go back. Here we are again in Sivas, then in Latakia, where finally we see the Mediterranean again. We do not have to reserve places in advance on a galley; we have only to choose among the ships in the roadstead, and we will reach Genoa after a month of sailing.

If we had left on board a Venetian ship to tour around the Venetian colonies, our voyage would not have been shorter. We should have had to include the time spent in stops at the trading posts and the numerous military colonies stationed at intervals along the route for the protection of the *mude,* the Venetian fleet. As in the Genoese zone of influence, we should have been expected and welcomed by a consul or a representative of the commune who would have found a lodging for us and who would have presented to the local authorities the treaties which would reduce or wave aside entry and exit requirements. This official representative would also have furnished us with all the current information about the political situation and the state of the markets.

After this voyage to the east, we could have undertaken another to the west. For as early as the thirteenth century, the Italians had ventured on the ocean, skirting the coasts of Southern France and Spain and then France. Towards the beginning of the fourteenth century the Genoese Lanzarotto Malocello, having deliberately set his course beyond the Straits of Gibraltar towards Safi, reached the Canaries and landed on an island which from that time on and throughout the fourteenth century was called "Lanzerotta" on Italian and Moroccan charts.

But if I should propose to accompany you on an imaginary trip to all the places frequented by Italian merchants in France, Germany, Flanders, and England, I should have to trace a hundred itineraries in order to name the innumerable cities and towns to which these hardy voyagers traveled, sometimes by sea, sometimes by the river routes, less costly and less dangerous, but most often by covering immense distances on foot, on horseback, or by mule.

5. The Position of Italy in Europe from the End of the Fourteenth Century to the End of the Fifteenth

It was at the end of the fourteenth century that Italian expansion abroad reached its happiest phase. Later it ceased to develop and in fact declined slowly. But throughout almost two centuries and especially in the second half of the fourteenth century Italy continued to contribute to the advance of trade, its complex and varied participation rendered more and more intensive by the development of foreign markets and new commercial undertakings at home.

Subsequently, this exuberant activity, this dynamism that had assured Italy a clear supremacy in every domain, underwent a regression that reduced it to inactivity at the very moment when other nations were asserting themselves. Formerly this dynamism of the Italians had manifested itself in the bold and supple organization of the city, in which individual valor could affirm itself despite juridical obstacles. At that time, the political units of Europe staggered under the weight of organisms which were too vast and badly articulated. They had also been weakened by the struggles between the kings and their vassals. This state of things naturally favored the Italian merchants in all their economic enterprises. By their initiative they had supplemented the insufficiencies of the financial organization; they had even furnished the sovereigns, who were anxious to restore and reaffirm their prestige, with the means to put their political programs into effect.

Later this situation underwent a complete reversal. It started when the monarchs could avail themselves of better managed resources and of large and well-equipped armies, which put them in a position to orient, organize, and defend their national market. To compete on an equal footing then, the Italians should have rid themselves of their ancient spirit of separatism; but they had learned only how to pass from the separatism of the city to that of the region. Later an even severer blow to their activity was the displacement of the axis of commercial traffic from the basin of the Mediterranean, the center of civilization since ancient times, to the Atlantic route that the Italians themselves had inaugurated, in the service, and to the benefit, of foreign powers.

For more than fifty years, however, the repercussions of this capital even were not too serious for Italy. It is the Italy of precisely that period that presents to the historians that euphoria to which I just alluded. The entry of new peoples and new territories into the economic game, the multiplication of credit money, and the new abundance of precious metals which had always been extremely rare—all this contributed to increase the demand on the part of more and more numerous classes of consumers, whose tastes and purchasing power determined the creation of new industries. In addition, the manufacture of extremely costly luxury goods catered to the growing pomp and splendor of the princes and the very wealthy. Both applied art and pure art knew a moment of unequalled prosperity. It was then that the Italians, who were no longer in the first rank in the production of woolen or cotton textiles, took a leading position in the making of silks.

This industry had originated in Sicily and, in the twelfth century, at Lucca. From there it had spread to Florence, Bologna, Milan, Genoa, and Venice, absorbing great numbers of workers and invading the markets, even to the point of dominating the market of Lyon. There was also a rapid development in woodworking, glassmaking, and in the processing of all the metals used in the manufacture of arms. Italian laces, Italian embroideries, Italian goldsmiths' work acquired a renown which soon became worldwide. Italian artists were called to foreign countries to build palaces, to design fortresses, to make statues, and to create frescoes and paintings. Thus a second wave of emigration took place, greater in extent than the first emigration at the time of the Crusades. Those who had crossed the frontier maintained from afar close ties with the mother country, to whom they were a source of wealth and pride. The merchant-bankers continued their traditional activity with a new advantage. In the past their principal goal had been to find, in the Orient, the products and raw materials which they could sell in markets of the Latin and Germanic world. These same merchants could find in the markets of the West numerous and varied products to fill the holds of their ships for the return trip. They had the further advantage of participating, if they desired, in all the enterprises destined to exploit the New World. And as numerous traders of many nationalities took part in the intermediary operations of buying and selling, the Italians chose to steer their capital into banking operations.

Their field of action was again extended to England. The transaction that took place between the Bardi and Richard II should suffice to prove that the company of that name remained in London. Documents tell us that after a hiatus, Italian commercial activity was resumed, especially the trade in jewelry and objets d'art. At the end of the fourteenth and during the course of the fifteenth century, the company of Filippo Borromeo (whose central office was in Milan) and the company of the Medici of Florence continued to import British wools to the continent.

The Italians also continued to live in France, which was soon to be the country of Catherine and Marie de' Medici. They settled mostly in Paris, which had become, under Charles V and Charles VI, a center of luxury and culture, and in Lyon, a city which Louis XI had made a center of commerce of the first rank and to which the fairs of Champagne had moved in the fifteenth century. In these two cities we find solidly established in the fifteenth century the Arnelfini, the Balbani, the Bonvisi, the Bondelmonti, the Burlamacchi, the Capponi, the Cenami, the Del Bene, the Frescobaldi, the Sardini, and the Guadagni, so rich that their name was often used as a synonym of wealth. After the battle of Pavia, Tommaso Guadagni lent 50,000 gold ducats to the king of France, out of his fortune of 400,000, which was the equivalent of five million pre-1914 liras.

After their long participation in the commercial and financial life of the fairs, the Italians prepared to devote themselves exclusively to banking, a specialization made possible by the power of their capital, their credit, and their knowledge in this field. They asserted themselves in this new domain toward the end of the fifteenth century and during the sixteenth at Lyon as well as at Besançon, Chambéry, Piacenza, and Novi-Liguria. Henry II received, 1,254,810 ducats from the "Florentine nation" when he found himself at war with the Spaniards; a Genoese company furnished him with 1,330,000 ducats, a company from Lucca with 730,737 ducats, and a Milanese company with 29,390. In the opposing camp, which the Fuggers of Augsburg subsidized heavily, Charles V obtained from Carlo Affaitati of Cremona the sum of 100,000 ducats. Other sums greater than this were turned over to him by Florentine bankers. Similarly, in the Brabant and in Flanders, many years went by before the Lombards were replaced by the Crespins and the Lochards. Tommaso Portinari, an agent of the Medici, was banker to Charles the Bold of Burgundy, then to Maximilian, who awarded him the receivership of the market tolls of Gravelines.

However, the colonial empires of Genoa and Pisa were gradually forced to abandon their positions—but Venice maintained hers by means of a long and tenacious resistance. The Italian trade losses were not sufficiently counterbalanced, especially in eastern central Europe and in northwestern Europe. In the first of these areas, with the exception of the territory that is now the Swiss Confederation, the Italians preferred to concentrate on managing the mines. In the second, they turned towards banking operations. In Fribourg and Geneva they continued to be moneylenders. In 1445 Antonio da Saliceto, inscribed on the lists of the local bourgeoisie, was taxed on the basis of 20,-300 liras, the equivalent of 400,000 gold francs of 1913, according to the Swiss scholar, Aebischer.

Finally, from the time when the colonies of the Black Sea flourished, Poland, which had been visited by Italian merchants since the thirteenth century, experienced a veritable invasion of Genoese, followed by citizens of Lucca, Bologna, Florence, and Venice. The period from 1333 to 1434 (the reign of Casimir the Great to that of Ladislaw II) can be considered as the most propitious for these merchants. After these years of prosperity, decline set in, brought on by various causes: the colonies of Kaffa and

Tana broke away; the anticlerical policies of the Jagellons alienated the bankers of the Pope charged with collecting tithes; and the Fuggers, who carried on these same functions in Germany, extended their field of action to Poland.

During the period that favored the success of Italian expansion, the salt marshes of the Cracow region, those of Bochnia and Vielickza, as well as those of the regions of Leopoli, Dohobicz, Dolina, and Przmisi, were administered by Italian *suppari*, who in their capacity as mayors, played a considerable part in the mining legislation of 1368.

If I have asked you to come with me on this voyage across the long centuries and through vast territories, it was in order to evoke the whole canvas of Italian commercial activity in the Middle Ages and to supplement the unilateral vision that Werner Sombart has given us, so that the particularly important role that Italy was called upon to play in the Middle Ages may be truly appreciated.

Chapter Four

THE SOURCES

W<small>E CAN GROUP</small> the documents concerning the economic history of the Middle Ages, and of Tuscany, into legislative texts, notarized documents, merchants' account books, and correspondence.

1. The Statutes

Medieval laws are to be found collected in the statutes elaborated by the councils of the guilds or by the municipal authorities. From the point of view of economics, the former are richer. But the latter have the additional interest of showing us the role of the state in the guild system. These laws underwent continual modification, as was necessary for a rapid adaptation to an ever-changing situation. This explains the variety and the quantity of the existing statutes, which would be even more numerous if many had not been destroyed.

However, these statutes, even though they are dated, present many problems of interpretation. Occasionally, following a revision of the law, the text was recopied in a new book, with a notation for the original year and the month. More often the original text was reused, because parchment was expensive. Corrections were made by means of erasures, marginal annotations, and overwriting; so that after several revisions the original text became almost illegible. Consequently, we are unable today to establish the chronology of the changes.

For other reasons, the analysis of the statutes must be undertaken with care. The Middle Ages would seem to be that period in history when the regulations in matters economic reflect least faithfully the realities they were designed to control. More than in any other epoch, theory and tradition are in conflict with the exigencies of life. On the one hand, profound, even excessive, aspirations toward continuous progress; on the other, moral principles imposed by the Church, which refused to follow those innovations it deemed too swift or those capable of overturning the social structure. The force of these moral strictures was such that the public powers had to resort to ruses to circumvent them. The most striking case is that of usury. At that time, this word was taken to mean any advantage whatsoever received in exchange for a loan. When the Church, through the Holy Fathers, had prohibited interest to be taken on capital loaned out, it had thought especially of loans intended to cover those expenses absolutely necessary—the purchase of food or the payment of tithes. With the development of commerce, this interdiction became a veritable anachronism; but the Church remained inflexible toward the merchant, in spite of all. So he had only two options: to submit and renounce splendid hopes, or to revolt. But revolt seemed impossible, as much from conscientious scruples as from fear of authority. Very naturally, the merchant found himself pushed to search the law which he himself had made for ways out, which would favor his ambitions without compromising his soul.

This conflict between law and reality, which in the case of usury took a particularly acute form, showed itself more or less clearly in all sectors of the economy. The statutes, for example, prohibited competition between fellow members of a guild. Here we see manifest the determination to make participants equal in order to maintain them in their initial equality. If these interdictions had been respected, if the distribution of raw materials between the business houses had been uniform, if the price of the finished products had remained identical (through a detailed regulation at each stage of the work), all the workshops and the stores would have kept an identical form and an equal power. But on the contrary, we find a whole hierarchy, from the smallest establishments up to the great Florentine companies of the Bardi, the Peruzzi, and the Acciaiuoli, who constituted a veritable trust, controlling or assimilating other business houses.

Furthermore, the guild regulations required anyone who practiced a profession or a trade to be a member of a guild. The public law repeated this obligation and reinforced it with the authority of the state. Each time the statutes were revised, the penalties became heavier for those who disobeyed. The insistence and the rigidity of the laws reveal the frequency of the infractions. But they could not be stopped, and nonmatriculated artisans continued to work quite openly. However, they had to submit to the rules of the guild and could not escape its control. The guild knew them and tolerated their names on its membership lists. But they could not take part in the council which directed its affairs.

Thus the economic development of Italy in the early Middle Ages attained a level unknown elsewhere, thanks to the violation of the rules that shackled it. Capitalism found its impetus in the peninsula, without a doubt; but we would look in vain for traces of its first steps in the statutes of the guilds. It is not a question of casting these documents aside, but of analyzing them with care; for they contain the elements of the dramatic struggle between the forces of the past and the forces of progress, or in other terms, the proof of the irresistible thrust of economic reality.

2. Notarized Documents

The *protocolli* of the notaries, of which we have some important collections, constitute another valuable source of information. We have about 1100 apiece from Genoa and Florence, and they are of an extraordinarily varied content. Despite what one may think, medieval man, more than any other, felt the necessity to write or to have someone write for him. He used the notary for numerous transactions, even minor ones, such as small loans, pledges on personal property, and agreements between a shopkeeper and his clerk, or a painter and his client. All this was registered! The *protocolli* are the books in which the notaries transcribed their contracts or *imbreviature*. The expression *incipit* marked the beginning of their very long and complicated formulae. A *protocollo* of one hundred pages may contain several hundred *imbreviature*.

The visit to the notary took place as follows: the clients stated the purpose of their business in the presence of witnesses; the man of law took notes and then proceeded to draft the contract—the *carta compiuta*—on a piece of legalized parchment bearing his name and his seal. If the contracting parties were nonmerchants and the agreement of minor importance, they usually dispensed with the final step, in order to save heavy expenses. The simple *imbreviatura* cost relatively little, but the registered document was expensive, because of the cost of the material as well as the honorarium for the scribe. Moreover, the latter document was executed especially when further contests at law were anticipated. The merchant wanted to have documents that would establish his rights before the judges, following the advice of Paolo di Messer Pace da Certaldo, who wrote in the fourteenth century: "When you make any paper whatever, in order to avoid a bad case and the dangers of false men, you should always have it completed and keep it well hidden in your strongbox."

One must use the notarized documents, like the legislative texts, with a great deal of circumspection. Do not forget that even today when someone seeks out a notary, he often tries to hide something from him. And this would have been more often the case in the Middle Ages, when it was necessary to avoid the condemnation of the Church. Sometimes figures are juggled today to avoid taxes, but the medieval merchant frequently altered the substance of the document. For example, a rapid examination of the *protocolli* gives the clear impression that real property never turned over so fast as in the Middle Ages, so numerous are the deeds of sale for houses and land. But if one digs below the surface, one sees that most of the time it is a question of something entirely different from a transfer of real estate. Here, in brief, is what often happened: Peter lent Paul a hundred florins, for which Paul put up as security a property greater in value than the face value of the loan, plus the interest. Peter engaged to return this property upon payment of the debt, after an agreed-upon delay. If this set of operations had been the subject of one single document, the truth would have been easily perceived and would have entailed grave consequences for the merchant. The danger seemed less if several documents were used for the transaction. One concerned the loan and stated the sum plus interest and the due date. Another stipulated, without alluding to the previous one, a sale of property *sic et simplicitur* between the borrower and the lender for a sum corresponding to the loan. In a third, the lender, without appearing as such, undertook to cede back to the borrower the property in question for the same amount of money. The transaction was therefore a loan, secured by a fictitious sale of property. As a further precaution, the three contracts were not registered at the same time nor with the same notary. So even the sharpest eyes of a potential censor could not have discovered the ruse; indeed, it misled the historians for a long time.

Therefore the inexperienced investigator examining the *protocolli* and the diplomatic parchments comes to the conclusion, already acquired from a superficial study of the statutes, that the merchants of the Middle Ages conformed to the dictates of the Church and to the legislature that reflected its principles; but this is very far from being the truth of the matter.

3. Commercial Records

The mercantile sources include the *libri di commercio* and the manuals or practical handbooks, to which we may add the personal memoirs or journals. Unfortunately, many of these documents have not survived, and we regret that, of those that have survived, the most common is the "secret book." In the Middle Ages each business house kept a number of records of the most diverse kinds. Naturally they varied according to the volume and complexity of the business of the house. This lack of uniformity is due in part to the absence of any law requiring the keeping of accounts, a situation to which attention was turned only later. The mass of huge ledgers and little scraps of memoranda, which today we would consider excessive, came about also because of the relative imperfections of their accounting systems; hence the necessity to exercise multiple controls. The accounts were repeated, not only in the figures, but in their details; and this in several separate books. The only record that we constantly find today is the famous "secret book," in which the director of the house, or the chief accountant in his place, entered everything that was necessary to establish at each and every point in time the position of the *compagni:* that is to say, the partners and the employees, who were called *fattori* ("factors") and *discepoli* ("clerks"), according to the functions they exercised. This "secret book" contains the original text, or a copy thereof, of the constitution of the company, whether it had been adopted under private seal or in front of a notary. We also find there each partner's share in the capital fund, the total amounts deposited by outsiders, the distribution of profits and losses at the close of each transaction, and finally the wages paid to the employees. The other books enlighten the historian on the activities of these men of affairs, but we easily understand why the medieval merchants guarded the "secret book" with the greatest care, while they dispersed or destroyed the others. The company could in fact come to an end, either through voluntary dissolution or through bankruptcy. Then the rights of outside investors were figured in the "notebooks of the syndics of receivers of the commune," but in this case too, the necessity was felt of keeping the only book that specified the obligations of the partners in the face of a liquidation that was frequently prolonged.

We also possess copies of certain important registers such as the *libre dell'asse*, about which many fantastic tales have been told. In reality they were only voluminous ledgers bound between two boards, since a parchment binding could not encompass its numerous pages. They began with an opening balance, restating the items of the budget contained in the *libro della ragione* and including the debits and credits of the company. They were presented to the company as open accounts, with its "payable" and "receivable" columns, and their counterparts, receivable and payable, in the open accounts under the names of the creditors and debtors of the company. These accounts were supplemented by two other groups: the "profits" and the "losses," corresponding to the active and the passive. Sometimes we also find the "cash book", the *livre de traites,* which today we would call "current accounts." I could cite others, differently set up according to the different commercial houses: for example, the "book for the branch house," for "purchases" and "sales" made in the warehouses, for "raw materials," for "domiciled workers," for "outside deposits," etcetera.

Their historical value is naturally determined by their veracity. No merchant was obliged to keep them; custom alone imposed them. But since the habit of recording commercial operations was widespread, the "statutes" dictated the rules to follow in keeping them in the best possible way. These rules varied according to the guild and the city, but they all endeavored to make any attempted deceit almost impossible. For example, the *partite* ("entries") had to be recorded in chronological order; erasures were admitted only if the word being corrected was still legible.

One could neither scratch out a mistake, nor bleach it out, but merely cross it out with strokes of the pen, and the corrections were either put above the cancellation or in the margins with a caret. In the Middle Ages, as in all ages, there was a temptation to falsify the books, except as concerns interest, a difficulty that the law itself ingeniously helped to overcome. The law in effect laid down this piece of good advice: never set down in writing that accursed word, but replace it with "gift" or some synonym proving that it was not a question of a *pactum firmum* imposed by the creditor, but a spontaneous token of gratitude on the part of the debtor. In order not to remove itself too far from the exigencies of the times, the Church contented itself with this fiction, except when the usury was too evident (as on the occasion of a lawsuit). Then, as now, fraud was limited by the difficulty of foreseeing, at the moment of recording a transaction, what form it would take in the future and by the fact that any subsequent modification of the records was made difficult by the obligation to keep chronological entries and by the prohibition on erasures. Furthermore, the merchant lived in the constant hope of a happy development of affairs; he invoked the protection "of God, of the Holy Virgin Mary, and of all the saints of the eternal life" upon the house, the partners, and the books. But this solemn precaution instilled fear and awe and to some degree precluded recourse to altering the books. After beginning by keeping honest records, it was thought not fitting to falsify, by a ruse easy to uncover, an instrument that testified to so many profitable operations. We can therefore have more confidence in the commercial books than in all the sources so far described, on the condition, however, that we keep our eyes open.

4. Merchants' Letters

The letters of the merchants are more trustworthy. Unfortunately, they are not numerous and there is very little in their content that can be fruitfully used; for one would have to possess whole series of letters and not isolated examples; but such groups are extremely rare. Their rarity, however, is compensated for by their variety. In most cases the merchant's letter represents more than a simple show of civility—it took the place of the modern newspaper. We find commercial information alternating with mathematical formulas, political information and dry figures, historical personages, comments on events of all sorts giving the measure of the culture of the writer, agreeable narratives of intrigues at the courts of lay or churchly princes, and gossip about people of secondary importance.

From this point of view, business records and correspondence can be used by several disciplines to embellish historical research with many interesting discoveries. In the course of reading these books and these letters, scholars have come across personages already cited by Boccaccio and Sacchetti and have been able to reconstruct their genealogies. It is there that we found the only character of the *Divine Comedy* not yet identified; and it is in an early fourteenth century account book that we learned what Petrarch's real name was. We can also correct the accepted opinion according to which the poet changed his original name from Petracchi to Petrarca, because it had a softer sound. As a matter of fact, when the accountant for the Frescobaldi Company noted down the increased salary of Ser Petrarca, his son Francesco, the future poet, was only eight years old.

5. *Commercial Handbooks*

We can easily form an idea of the manuals from the title page of the one that is most famous. It carries the name of Francesco di Balduccio Pegolotti, one of the managing directors of the Florentine company of the Bardi in the fourteenth century. We read in the preface: "This book is called the book of indications of weights and measures of merchandise and of other things that merchants in different parts of the world need to know. This book contains information on goods and currencies and the relations between the goods of one country and another and of one land and another. At the same time, it will show how to tell which are the best goods, where they come from, and how they can be preserved as long as possible."

And from the introduction to Chiarini's manual: "Here begins a book about all the customs, the moneys, the weights, the measures, and the rules for bills of exchange, and the terms employed in the letters of exchange which are used in the different countries and the diverse lands." The handbooks dealt with merchandise produced and traded and with the rules of trade. They give equivalent weights and measures, the currencies used and their exchange rates, details of the costs of voyages and transport, imposts and duties of every kind that had to be paid to the princes, the lords, and the cities for the movement of goods, and finally, information on commercial customs. These are all things that we do not find so easily in other documents, and never grouped in this systematic fashion. In the manuals we also find formulas that permitted the accountant to do his calculations rapidly. As concerns the changing of money, they furnish not only the current rate and recent fluctuations, but also a table of previous varia-

tions. In addition they contain procedures for refining and
alloying gold and silver, preserving for us some rare reci-
pes. And finally we find in the handbooks some excellent
tables that constitute a sort of perpetual calendar.

The foundation for these works was multiple. First, the
experience of the compiler in the course of his own voyages and the information given him by his correspondents.
But the compilers also consulted the archives of the guilds,
so that we have set before us a panorama of the period,
gleaned from papers now dispersed or destroyed. In arith-
metical matters, they had recourse to scholarly treatises, of
which the most ancient is that of Leonardo Pisano. The
treatises constituted a whole didactic apparatus of questions
and answers, of methods of operation, which had to be
adapted to more practical ends. These trade manuals were
composed by the merchants themselves, not by erudites or
specialists. That is why they fit so well the requirements of
the times. That is why there is not just one single text, but
a whole series of versions each with different dimensions. If
there were, for example, two mercantile companies, one
with branches and businesses in fifty markets, the other in
liaison with only ten, the first felt the need of assembling
greater amounts of information, the other a more limited
quantity.

We have, then, a difference and variety in size, but not
a remarkable difference in content. Almost all these commercial handbooks shared a common content; sometimes
whole passages were identical.

We are astonished, arrested by an apparent contradic-
tion. How can we reconcile the secrecy of the medieval
business houses with the relative uniformity of these precious instruments, the practical handbooks? We can explain
the identity of some passages by an identity of sources: for

example, the text of a royal ordinance or an article from the statutes.

In other cases we can suppose that the directors of the companies, who were the authors of the handbooks, could move—and in fact they did move—from one mercantile house to another. In that case they naturally took with them a copy of their work or that of their fellow directors, or at the very least, numerous notes which they used in their new business life. Another reason for this uniformity could be the dissolution and reconstitution under another name of certain commercial houses.

These practical handbooks are to be found in libraries, and especially in private archives, occasionally in state archives. The longest ones have been printed, since they were thought to be the most important and therefore would be consulted more. But it is surely unnecessary to insist on the value of these documents, since they are clearly the basic tool of the economic historian.

6. *Memoirs and Journals*

The memoirs take their place among the literary texts and the economic sources by virtue of their extraordinary richness of content and beauty of form, which has gained them the honor of detailed literary analysis. We have already spoken of the tendency of the medieval man, particularly the businessman, to write or to have someone write for him on all that took place around him. Thus the merchant sets down in his memoirs all the political facts of his city and information reported to him in person by returning travelers; sometimes he adds his own observations. So we get a sort of chronicle of the century, not at all insignificant, even though not comparable to the most famous chronicles. Of course we find in the memoirs the more homely details: marriages, dowries, births, and the costs of rearing and educating the children; deaths and the costs of funerals; agreements between the companies, celebration banquets, and when the occasion warranted, tilting matches and tourneys. Housekeeping details are recorded in the memoirs; even sometimes the day-to-day expenditures for food. The merchant freely notes the sums he has paid in taxes, his relations with the business house in which he is a partner, or his private transactions: the sale or purchase of property, the giving or taking of loans, and more freely still, details of delicate business affairs that he has embarked upon. Prudence dictates that he make some notes, first for himself—one cannot trust one's memory—or for his heirs, if they should suddenly succeed to the management of his affairs. Such is the counsel of Paolo di Messer Pace di Certaldo, whom we cited above. "Always, when you have a paper drawn up, have a book of your own and inscribe in this book the date, the name of the notary who registered the document, and the witnesses; write also the import of the document, so that your children, if they have need of it, can find it." And the historian in his turn can profit from this advice, as when he finds the names of the different notaries who employed their art and their authority in the service of a merchant who wanted to disguise a loan (or rather the interest on that loan) by a purchase and a sale with right of repurchase.

The personal memoirs are therefore sources of the first order, not only for the information they contain, but for the confidence with which we can accept them. Meant only for the eyes of the man who wrote them, or for his children and heirs, they were composed with a sincerity founded on the certain knowledge that they were sheltered from any outside scrutiny.

7. *Chronicles*

The best-known chronicles, those of Giovanni Villani, interest us particularly, because they are filled with a remarkable number of those facts that today we call statistics. We know what a chronicle is: a narrative that we place between the work of the analyst, which it surpasses by its greater elaboration of information, and that of the historian, whose level it does not reach. In the naïve simplicity of its reasoning, all real criticism is absent, except that which is the spontaneous fruit of the mind and soul of the author, or too often, of his passions as the man of one faction or another, a rather feeble assurance of his fidelity to history. To what extent can we, and should we, believe in the chronicles? Undoubtedly, the historian should address himself to them as a last resort, after having completed his researches on the basic documents. But when he is forced to resort to them for want of other sources of information, he should divest himself of the blind faith of the nineteenth century scholars, as well as the scepticism of certain historians of our own century, and sharpen his critical senses to the maximum.

It is interesting to report the result of control exercises that have been done to ascertain the veracity of the two great chroniclers, the Venetian Marin Sanudo and the Florentine Giovanni Villani, by comparing their data with the original documentation. As for Sanudo, the figures he reports on the finances of the Republic have found "an easy and sure verification in the official texts." In the domain of

commerce, discussion is possible. Sanudo states that at the
beginning of the fifteenth century the republic annually
used 10,000,000 ducats for its foreign trade; our information gives us the figure of 9,600,000 ducats. But we must
consider that the exemptions granted to several foreign
merchants leave a large enough margin so that the chronicler's assertion may not be unreasonable. The same conclusions apply to Villani, for the period discussed, that is to say,
1336–1341. Florence reached the apogee of her power at
that moment, as did Venice at the start of the fifteenth century. The figures Villani gives for the revenues from the
octrois (300,000 florins per annum) are exact, as is the
amount of the commune's debt for public loans (100,000
florins on July 15, 1336; 400,000 in 1341; 800,000 at the
end of 1342). However, for the sum consolidated in the institution of the *Monte*, our reconstruction from the documents gives the figure of 505,044 florins as against 570,-
000 indicated by the chronicler. Nevertheless, Villani was
in a position to obtain exact figures, or very close to it, because several times, in conjunction with other citizens, he
was a director of municipal finances, and he was frequently
consulted by those "merchants wise and subtle" who were
charged with public duties at the same time he was. By the
same token we can also accept his data on commerce: on
the number of wool shops and the number of pieces of cloth
produced and their value. Villani had the opportunity of
getting his information from sources that were both sure
and complete, that is to say, the archives of the guilds and
the mouths of the merchants themselves. For he knew all
these merchants, and he was particularly linked with several of them, his associates in the company to which he belonged. On the other hand, Villani exaggerates when he
states that the sum Edward III owed to the Bardi and the

Peruzzi, in the middle of the fourteenth century at the time of the famous collapse, was 1,365,000 gold florins, which, as he said, "was worth a kingdom." But this time the author did not have precise information at his disposal. The business books, especially on the eve of the catastrophe, did not reflect the entire truth; they were not complete. And the situation did not become much clearer subsequently, in the course of the difficult liquidation, because the English authorities sequestered all the accounts of the realm, and at the same time the administrators and directors in Florence hid all the books and registers they possessed, interested as they were in concluding settlements *in loco* rather than having to accept unlimited and collective responsibility toward their creditors *en masse*. And finally, another factor destroys Villani's figures: he could not foresee, at the time, the partiality of the foreign receivers and the refusal of the king to consider himself indebted not only for the sums he had received, but also for those that he had promised under the title of "gift." Now, of these sums promised, certain of them had been intended, at the time of their concession, as proof of gratitude for the "great favors that the king had received"; others represented disguised interest. Villani, then, could not tell the truth, and he did not tell it. But that does not authorize us to say that he had neither the desire nor the opportunity to be exact in his facts.

As to his demographic evidence, the present state of our knowledge does not permit us to make any judgments. We can only hope that the specialists will begin direct research with new methods, different from those (with few exceptions) very clumsy ones that have been used up to now.

In brief, the problem of the degree of confidence to accord Villani seems to present itself as follows: when the official documents on the facts that he reports have not come down to us, we must ask whether or not they existed in his time. If the response is affirmative, we may believe that he has consulted them and has used them with care, since we know he was a man endowed with a mind accustomed to the accuracy of accounting practices and with a culture whose quality often raised him from the level of a chronicler to the rank of an historian. Thanks also, I shall repeat, to his active participation in both the political and economic life of the city.

If the reply is negative, it should not be thought that Villani could put his hands directly on the relevant statistics. That would have been difficult for him, and sometimes impossible, even if he had wanted to. His statements in such cases are undoubtedly touched with fantasy, a fantasy moderated, however, by that sentiment of responsibility inveterate in him, which could not fail to protect him against exaggerations. It is true that his political passions and his ardent love of his native city pushed him, in spite of himself, to exalt its grandeur. But even when Villani's figures are approximate, the historian can have a certain confidence in them in shaping his idea of the economic life of fourteenth century Florence. On the whole, we can affirm that, in the absence of precise figures on medieval economy, the works of the important chroniclers are a very valuable source, one which should be used critically but one which it would be imprudent to renounce.

I have indicated above only the principal sources, especially those whose critical interpretation absolutely requires the aid of a guide. I have hardly spoken of the possibilities offered by a long list of documents: the series of state archives; the series of the consultations which reproduce the discussions preceding every administrative decision; the tax registers, from the "register of land surveys" to the "register of victuals" and the "register of wealth." I should add that the basement of many a building contains materials useful to the economic historian, such as the codes for the apprentices, the files of documents of the *Tribunal de la Mercanzia*, the archives of the guilds, the registers of lawsuits held before ecclesiastical magistrates, and so on. We cannot embark here on a full description of these sources. And a simple list would be useless and incomprehensible, since the terminology for analogous documents varies from city to city, so that it would be necessary to explain each case separately.

But that is all the more reason to hope that this simple work will be the point of departure for new and fruitful research. Here, in the setting of your new school, it is logical to abandon oneself to hope, to believe in the virtue of new conceptions of the historian's work. We shall no longer be restricted to the methods of the artisan, as we have been until now, in France, as in Italy. I hope therefore that the tremendous possibilities of contemporary studies will not absorb all of your labor but that you will apply some of it to that magnificent field—the economic life of the Middle Ages.